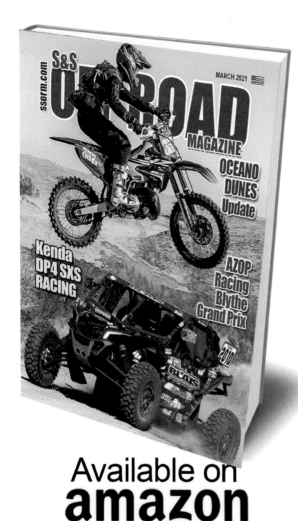
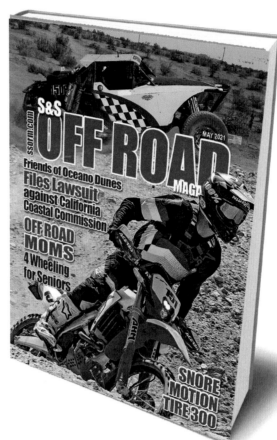
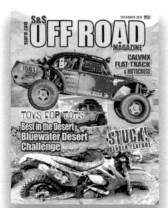
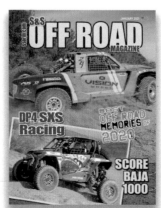

JUNE 2023 - VOL 41, NO. 9

FEATURES

COMPETITION

CONTENTS

#277 Micah Ross, seventh Pro Production and #444 Steve Nottoli, second Sportsman at the AMA District 38 OTB California 160, a UTV only desert race, April 15, 2023 in the Superstition OHV area near El Centro CA. Photo by Judd Neves Nothing But Dirt Racing Photography

COVER

TOP Robbo Pippin finished fifth Sportsman at the AMA District 38 OTB California 160 race, April 15, 2023. Photo by Judd Neves Nothing But Dirt Racing Photography BOTTOM Ryder Bitz-Hay finished second Open Unclassified at the Fast Friday Night Before Ventura race at Perris Raceway, May 5, 2023 presented by SCFTA Racing. Results and photos from that event will follow in the July issue of *S&S Off Road Magazine*. Photo by Hangar 53 Studios - www.hangar53studios.com

MORE RACING
Transaxle Engineering

Bronsen Chiaramonte finished
14th overall and 10th Class 10

April 29, 2023
Lucerne Valley CA
www.moreracing.net
Photos by RNR Race Photos

Challenge

Donny Donovan finished fifth Class 11 at the MORE Racing Transaxle Engineering Challenge in Lucerne Valley CA

Driver Kurt Youngs and co-driver Lukas Oliger.
"We had an amazing run going and ended up fifth for the day.
MORE puts on the best 1600 races and can't wait for the next one."

"The Transaxle Engineering Challenge course was a blast. We went out there and ran the truck hard, only having a couple issues but we managed to pull off the win. Thanks to Giant Motorsports, Deaver Springs, West Coast Converters, Mike's Transmission and Shock Tuning by KDM Shock Technologies." Owner/Driver Kyle Thomas, Co-Driver Scott Kuhn, first Class 2000

TOP TEN OVERALL HEAT 1 1. Mike Malloy (Class 1600) 2. Cole Hardin (Class 1600) 3. Kyle Ahrensberg (Class 2900) 4. Hunter Carpenter (Class 1600) 5. Jack Clinkenbeard (Class 1600) 6. Kurt Youngs (Class 1600) 7. Mikey Kelly (Class 600) 8. Brodie Martin (Class 1600) 9. Mark Carter (Class 600) 10. Brooke Perfect (Class 1600)

TOP TEN OVERALL HEAT 2 1. Jack Grabowski (Class 6100) 2. Shawn Croll (Class 1) 3. Eric Hardin (Unlimited Truck) 4. Bryce Farrar (Class 10) 5. Holden Heitritter (Class 10) 6. Roger Starkey (Class 10) 7. Ron Weddle (Class 10) 8. Dean Wheeler (Class 10) 9. John Bowers (Unlimited Truck) 10. Tom Coons (Class 10)

CLASS RESULTS - TOP FIVE

Class 10 1. Bryce Farrar 2. Holden Heitritter 3. Roger Starkey 4. Ron Weddle 5. Dean Wheeler

Class 1600 1. Mike Malloy 2. Cole Hardin 3. Hunter Carpenter 4. Jack Clinkenbeard 5. Kurt Youngs

Class 11 1. Daniel Boswell 2. Jeff Corrao 3. Mauro Diaz 4. Cole Wimmer 5. Donny Donovan

Class 2000 1. Kyle Thomas 2. Steven Olsewski 3. Dennis Gerdes 4. Tyler Pullen 5. Kevin Knight

Class 9 1. Jacob Wisdom 2. Todd Johnson 3. Tommy Phillips 4. Detrick Kelley

Class 1400 1. Jake Hamilton 2. Adam Leonhardt

Class 1400 Pro 1. Dustin Brodwolf 2. Brett Michael 3. Dan Fertal

Class 1900 1. Brandon Burns 2. Nick Masson 3. Dennis McBride

Class 2900 1. Kyle Ahrensberg 2. Ronnie Wilson

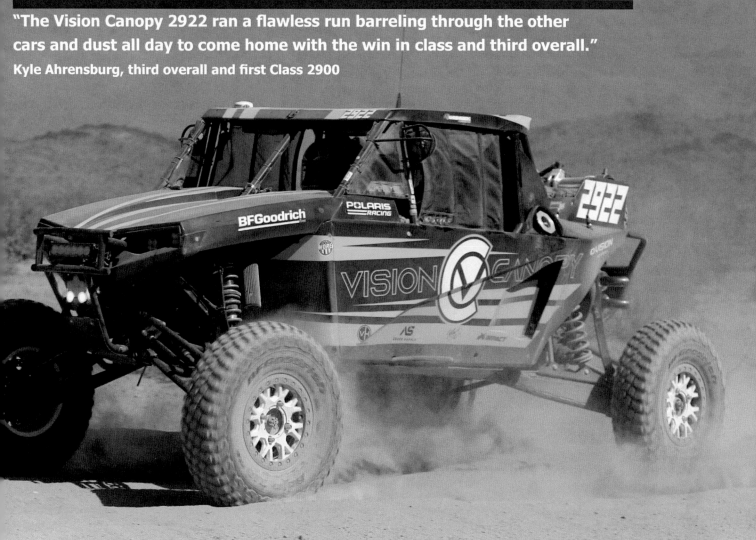

"The Vision Canopy 2922 ran a flawless run barreling through the other cars and dust all day to come home with the win in class and third overall."
Kyle Ahrensburg, third overall and first Class 2900

"Cody/MORE, put on a great race. The course was equal parts technical and fast. Unfortunately I broke a header at race mile 22 and had to return to the pits for a repair. We made it back out but at mile 6 of our second lap my alternator quit and we had to call it a day. I'm new to the sport and have learned so much. Slowly we are working out the bugs in my truck and I hope to finish a race soon. I'm a 55-year-old grandma of 4, racing with my niece as my co-driver. As the only females in our class we are having a great time and we hope to find some sponsorship to help us with equipment in the future." - Janis Miller, ninth Class 2000 at the Transaxle Engineering Challenge in Lucerne Valley, April 29, 2023

RNR RACE PHOTOS

FIND THE HIDDEN 10MM AND YOU JUST MIGHT WIN THIS 10MM SOCKET SET!

Donated by Spinning Wheels Photography

Input your answer online @ www.ssormag.com

Winner of the
May 2023 10mm Contest
SAMANTHA SUTTLE

Attention winner:
Send your mailing address to ssormag@gmail.com

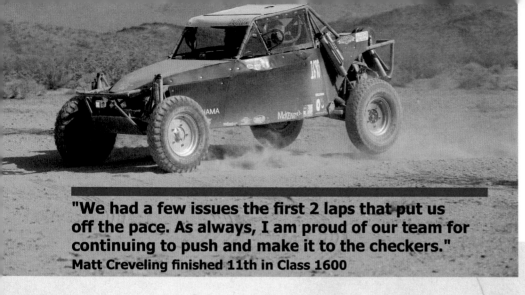

"We had a few issues the first 2 laps that put us off the pace. As always, I am proud of our team for continuing to push and make it to the checkers."
Matt Creveling finished 11th in Class 1600

Unlimited Truck 1. Eric Hardin 2. John Bowers 3. Vincent Klos
Class 1300 1. Bridget Minor 2. Robert Figlioli
Class 600 1. Mikey Kelly 2. Mark Carter
Class 5/1600 1. Conner Ishibashi 2. Sean Cope
Class 6100 1. Jack Grabowski 2. Chris Paxson
Class 1 1. Shawn Croll
Class 7200 1. Mike Shaffer

Bryce Farrar, first Class 10 and fourth overall in Heat 2

RNR RACE PHOTOS

Sean Cope, second Class 5/1600

RNR RACE PHOTOS

"The team headed to Lucerne valley April 28th to take on the Transaxle Engineering Challenge put on by M.O.R.E. Saturday came and Team Lacey started the race at about 8:30 am and got to mile 2 and lost complete power steering first lap, but did not give up. We just had to manage without it and we ended up making it back to the main pit where the pump was completely gone. Went off for our second lap and at mile 17 our third member exploded and that ended our day short." Nate Lacey finished eighth Class 2000

"Well we made it back home safe. Thank you everyone who came out to help! Chris Deans and family, Jono Liebrenz and Casey Benito. And everyone who helped Cody Jeffers/ MORE racing put on the Transaxle race this weekend. We DNF'd. First lap at mile 30 we were coming in hot, seen a G-out and stood on the brakes. Wasn't enough. We went flying! Rolled about 4 times! Landed on driver side. Made sure my co-driver was ok. I unbuckled, got out to check the situation. Course workers pulled us over and then off the track. Radio'd to my help to bring tires and oil. My wife Brittany Kelley and Chris Deans showed up. Changed 2 tires added oil, readjusted the mirrors and kept going. Got into the second lap and had a 16 car on our tail thru a single car canyon. Tried to get out of his way as fast as I could but nothing but ditch walls. Couldn't go nowhere but forward. Apparently he had somewhere to go. Lol. And bumped the &*#% out of me. Guessing it was my tire because not less than thirty seconds later I heard a clunking noise. Drove it out as much as I can. Six miles later I had no gears. Sooo yeah. Casey Benito rescued me. But it was awesome! Wouldn't trade that time for nothing else. Until the next time."
Detrick Kelley, Class 9 🚜

Sherri's Turn

"Can I buy that for you?"

I looked across the table at the man who never touched a computer in his life. He was listening to the guy-in-the-garage and I talk about my need for a laptop many years ago.

He knew we were traveling back and forth from home regularly to help as his health deteriorated. He knew without us saying so, that switching from a desktop computer to a laptop would help us get work done when we were away from home.

I looked over at him. He said it again.

"That computer you want. Can I buy that for you?"

Do you ever feel like a weight has just been lifted on your shoulders completely unexpectedly? It's a great feeling.

"Sure, you can buy it if you want to," I said.

He got his checkbook out, signed a blank check and shoved it across the table toward me. "How much do you need?"

This was the man who was not my dad. But he might as well have been and he was an awesome replacement for the one who had walked out on our family in my early teens.

I first met the man who would become my father-in-law when I was about 17. He had no daughters. I discovered being like a daughter had certain benefits. In his eyes, a daughter could do no wrong.

His boys, however, could do much wrong. Take the time he and his wife went out to eat and his sons and I decided that it would be fun to fly kites. A nice windy day. Then we realized it would be even more fun to fly them off the flat roof of his house. We were probably all still teenagers at the time.

When he arrived home, you could hear the roar for miles around it seemed, as he spotted his sons on the roof. "What are you doing on my roof?! You'll ruin it. You get off there . . . " and I don't know what all else he said. But then the brother-in-law-in-the-garage uttered the magic words. And I do mean magic.

"Sherri is up here, too."

They motioned for me to step over to the edge of the house so their dad could see me. So I did.

His whole demeanor changed. "Okay, well you be careful up there." Then he went in the house and never uttered another word about it.

He wasn't an off road dad who was involved in the sport, but he paved the way for his sons, when he bought them the first motorized toy for the dirt. A Powell Challenger mini bike. He drove them to the nearby canyons to ride it. As time passed, motorcycles came along. He bought one for

JUNE 2023 | VOL. 41 • NO. 9 | SINCE 1982 | ssormag@gmail.com | 760-336-1512 | **PUBLISHER** S&S Publishing Inc. **EDITORS** Steve Kukla - Sherri Kukla **EDITORIAL ASSISTANT** Summer Kukla **COLUMNISTS** Tom Severin - Ed Stovin **CONTRIBUTORS** Kathryn Caro | Steve Caro | Judd Neves | Neal Rideout Photography | RNR Photos | Scott Spinning | Trackside Photo | Jeff Waldaias | **IN MEMORY** C&C Race Photos - Carlos Avina | Roy Denner | Jim Ober | Harold Soens |

each of his two sons. That was in the 1960's. Over 50 years later they're still riding dirt bikes. But now there aren't just two bikes. Between the two of them there are probably 15 or 20 bikes. And no, Dad didn't buy those. In fact he probably would have thought it excessive. But in all fairness, he was the one who got them started.

He was a dad who provided. A dad who loved. A dad who never skipped out on his family. Who never put his own wants ahead of his kids

We said good-bye to this amazing man not long after the photo was taken. He was a giving man all the way to the end. A few months before he passed away, we had taken him to the emergency room. When the doctors decided to admit him, he said to us. "You don't have to stay. Get some money out of my wallet and stop and buy yourself dinner on the way home."

He's been on my mind as I put together the annual Off Road Dads feature. I love seeing all the men involved in the lives of their children. I'm reminded of a recent Zoom Bible study I was leading. It's made up of women I've met at the race track. I'm not even sure how this topic came up, but it turned out that none of us in the meeting this past week grew up with a committed loving father in our lives.

Researching the epidemic of fatherlessness I've discovered the sad fact that over 24 million children in the United States live without a father in their lives. That's 33% of children under the age of 18. And never mind, just under the age of 18, even when you're 28 or 38 or older, you still rely on a dad. We sure did on my father-in-law. He was a constant. Always available. Always loving. And we are

The guy-in-the-garage (AKA Steve), his dad and brother Ted, in 2008 recreating the picture they took when the bikes were new. Shown here with restored models of the same type of motorcycles their dad first bought them.

blessed for that. I am blessed to have had a father replacement such as him.

Which brings me to the point I want to make at this time of year when we honor our fathers. If you're a dad who is present in your children's lives, or even a man who doesn't have children, consider being there for fatherless children in your neighborhood or in your circle of friends. Step in and be that substitute dad for them.

And for those who are uninvolved dads, please consider changing that. Be there for your children. It will be the most important thing you ever do in your life.

Oh, and about being that daughter who could do no wrong in the eyes of my father-in-law. A few weeks before he passed away, while we were living with him and caring for him, apparently I fed him spaghetti once too many times and he yelled at me. He was sick of it.

I was stunned. In 35 years of knowing him he had never raised his voice at me. Not once. I was indignant and so tempted to say, "I am not one of your sons to be yelled at!"

But instead I looked at him and knew. I love this man. He has always been there for me. And that's a lot more than I can say for my own dad. 🏍

S&S OFF ROAD MAGAZINE is published monthly by S&S Publishing Inc., Ocotillo Wells CA 92004 (760) 336-1512; www.ssormag.com, ssormag@gmail.com. Reprinting in whole or in part expressly forbidden except by permission of the publisher. © 2023. We reserve the right to edit or reject any advertising and/or editorial copy. **ADVERTISING** Sherri Kukla (760) 336-1512 call/text or ssormag@gmail.com **BACK TO THE DESERT®** | **TEAR DOWN TIME® SAN DIEGO OFF ROADER® SAN DIEGO OFF ROAD MAGAZINE®** are registered trademarks of Steve and Sherri Kukla

AMA District 38
OTB California 160

"We started on the third row, got the Holeshot on our line and quickly caught the two lines ahead of us. We moved into the physical lead around mile 10 on the first lap and was able to settle into a smooth pace. We were able to take first overall by around 10 minutes in our Polaris Rzr Pro R." - Josh Row with co-driver Preston Axford, first 2000 N/A and first overall

Superstition OHV Area - El Centro CA
April 15, 2023
www.amad38.com
Photos by Judd Neves Nothing But Dirt Photography

"The D38 UTV series offers a wide range of opportunities for even the most green and conservative drivers. I purchased a brand new 2022 Wildcat from Coyne Powersports just two weeks prior to my first race. Even though we ended up splitting a front drive line component clean in half, myself and my Co-Driver Zach Goodbody had an excellent safe time. My two brothers and I are currently racing in the series and it has become an indispensable family affair coupled with competitive banter and recording stories to tell for seasons to come. Our tight group of friends and racers now have daily conversation about which tires to run and which shock settings work the best and who runs what oil in their engines. There seems to always be an outlet for the family when you need one during the D38 UTV series." - Cory Aymar, third Pro Stock

"D38 OTB California 160 was such a rad course. I knew it was bound to have a little bit of everything, from high speed sections to gnarly whoops. We stayed fast, consistent and made very little mistakes to keep Lobo alive. Thanks to all my sponsors that made this win possible!!" - Victor Rangel, first Pro Production Turbo, second overall

"It was my very first race as a driver, switching from the co-driver side and it was really fun! It was a great course. I am very honored that Wild Bill let me drive his car. I look forward to the rest of the season! Lots of work, time, and effort went into setting up the car and our pit crew at W.A.T. Racing was amazing. I couldn't have done it without any them. Most importantly my co-driver Wild Bill McNeer!" - Katelyn Singh, fourth Sportsman

TOP TEN OVERALL

1. Josh Row 2. Victor Rangel 3. Patrick Taber 4. Angel Aviles III 5. Jeff Hoskins 6. Brandon Rauch 7. Jaimes M. McKinney 8. Ryder Dennett 9. Will Salazar 10. Kayla Hopper

CLASS RESULTS - TOP FIVE

2000 NA 1. Josh Row 2. Harrison Weiss 3. Todd Barnhill

Pro Production Turbo 1. Victor Rangel 2. Patrick Taber 3. Angel Aviles III 4. Kayla Hopper 5. Brice Allen

"We had a lot of fun this last race. The track was laid out great for the SXS. We started on the second line in Pro Unlimited. By Coyote Wash we were first overall. Unfortunately we lost a belt right before the pits. We went through two more and we were forced to stop for lack of belts. Track was really sandy. Thanks OTB, we need more courses like that." - Christopher Hoffman, sixth Unlimited

Unlimited 1. Jeff Hoskins 2. Hilario Haro 3. Jeff Taylor 4. Stephen Frick 5. Chris Hoffman
Sportsman 1. Brandon Rauch 2. Steve Nottoli 3. Anthony Chavez 4. Katelyn Singh 5. Robert Pippin III
Pro Production 1. Jaimes M. McKinney 2. Ryder Dennett 3. Will Salazar 4. Darren Scott 5. Bob Leslie
Pro Stock 1. Rob Niemela 2. Bob Leslie 3. Cory Aymar

2440 LA MIRADA DR. VISTA, CA 92081
P: (760) 599-0090 & F: (760) 599-0070
WWW.CROWNPERFORMANCE.COM
SALES@CROWNPERFORMANCE.COM

STAINLESS STEEL BRAKE LINES

DIRECT AND CUSTOM FIT LINES FOR AUTOS, TRUCKS AND SUVs

- D.O.T. Approved
- Five (5) Layer Brake Line
- Eight (8) Colors Available

- Oil, Fuel & A/C Lines
- Power Steering Lines
- Liquid & Cooling Lines
- Clutch & Hydraulic Lines
- Shock & Suspension Lines

- Custom Lengths & OEM Replacements
- No Expansion/Immediate Pedal Response
- Fittings & Adapters For All Types Of Sizes & Threads

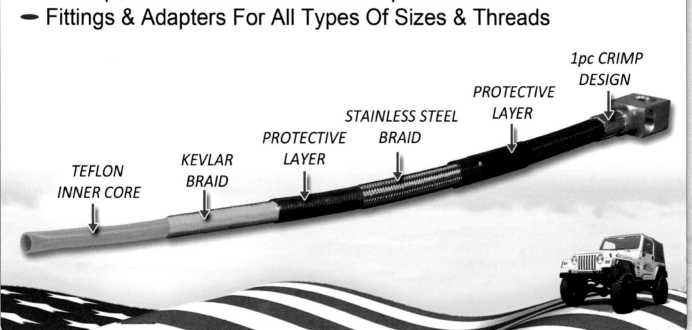

TEFLON INNER CORE
KEVLAR BRAID
PROTECTIVE LAYER
STAINLESS STEEL BRAID
PROTECTIVE LAYER
1pc CRIMP DESIGN

JUDD NEVES PHOTOS

"We had a great race except for a few issues on lap one that cost us a couple minutes, but we got it all figured out and put our Bachar Performance built engine to the test and charged forward for a second in class. Special thanks to my co-driver Mark Hernandez and my family for always supporting." - Ryder Dennett, second Pro Production, eighth overall

A LITTLE DIRT NEVER HURT

Mention This Ad To Recieve a Special Offer

Email Mike@visualimpactpro.com
OR
Call 951.928.4280

TENTS · TABLE COVERS · FLAGS · AND MORE

VISUAL IMPACT PROMOTIONS

JUDD NEVES PHOTOS

Jaimes McKinney, first Pro Production, ninth overall

Hilario Haro, second Pro Unlimited, sixth overall

OFF ROAD DADS

Here's a picture of my dad, John Gronek, working on the bike in Ventura before practice.
- LJ Gronek, G&G Racing

Racing is more fun when you compete with your Dad! Blake, Chad and Wyatt.
- Kristi Reed, El Centro CA

OFF ROAD DADS

A photo from when my husband, David, and our son, Dylan, raced with AZOP. They had a few great years of racing together! - Jamie Tomkins, Lakeside AZ

Monte is an off road dad to me and my older brother Melvin. He started off road racing since before we were born. We grew up with it. He has won multiple championships throughout the years, and will be chasing another one this next year. Not only is he an exceptional driver, he has built all of his trucks from start to finish including the new hot commodity #1456 his little brother, Jason Bettelyoun's, truck. It doesn't matter if we are in the desert or the mud we love all of the off-roading! We support our dad in off roading by being his co drivers and helping out wherever we can. We just love being a part of the off-road sport! - Monica Tibbitts, Yuma AZ.

Mark "Saby" Arguilez Jr with his dad Mark Arguilez. Saby getting back on the bike in March 2020 after recovering from his broken arm in December of 2019.
- Victtoria Leon, Campo CA

Kayla Hopper with dad Doug Hopper at a District 38 desert race

OFF ROAD DADS

Tyler and 14 year old Mack Stewart of Las Vegas NV before the SNORE Battle at Primm race, where they won the unlimited UTV class in their Polaris Pro R.

Art Mondragon with his daughter Auberi - Sheila Gervais, La Quinta CA

OFF ROAD DADS

My dad, Doug McPheeters, in his happy place. Photo by son, Jesse McPheeters, El Cajon CA

Here is a shot of my son Wyatt Bernard and I after taking first place at the 2022 Yerington 250 in our 1600 car. He helps prep the car, and cheers dad from the pits. Someday this will be his car and we will switch places.
- Heath Bernard, Reno NV

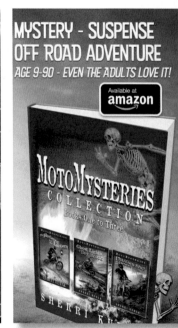

Loren and Danny Duncan, Buttercup 1982

Steve Kerchner and son Nathan out on a ride at Superstition in April. - Tracy Kerchner, Alpine CA

This is Mike "The Pigfarmer" Cuff at Surprise, Arizona doing his Yamaha RMAX Adventures for Yamaha Motorsports, his part-time job.

So many great photos and more importantly memories of dad. Very hard to choose just one. Dad made me who I am today. He gave me my first start in Off- Road Racing in 1977, I was 17. And hey I'm still doing it. Dad was a man's man. Always in charge and always on top of everything. He is with God now in Heaven. I miss him every day. - Dave Simpson, Corona CA

1st Annual OFF-ROAD JAMBOREE

FROM RACE TRUCKS TO ROCK CRAWLERS
COME SUPPORT

DATE: SATURDAY JUNE 24TH, 2023

TIME: 11AM-7PM

LOCATION: LAKESIDE RODEO GROUNDS

GENERAL ADMISSION $20

VIP BBQ ENTRY $40

KIDS 12 & UNDER FREE

MUST REGISTER ONLINE AT

WWW.SDORC.ORG

VIP BBQ PROVIDED BY

Fern's Semi-Famous BBQ

MUST PREREGISTER FOR
VIP BBQ BY 6-17-23

EL CAJON HOBBIES

EL CAJON HOBBIES WILL BE BUILDING A RC TRACK
INSIDE LAKEIDE RADEO AREA COMPLETE WITH A
FUN OBSTACLE COURSE & FASTEST LAP WINS PRIZE

BRING YOUR OWN RC CAR
TO COMPETE FOR FASTEST LAP

Dad Tim Morenc and Son Jake Morenc mid-ride at the Stillwater 500 in Oklahoma.

OFF ROAD DADS

Dad John Gill, Son David Gill, and photo taken by Trail Lead Tim Morenc at the Stillwater 500 in Oklahoma.

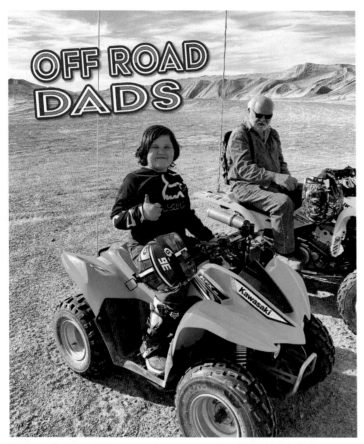

OFF ROAD DADS

My dad, Greg Rice, and my son Paul Rice. He's been an off road dad since the early 1980's
- Will Rice, Westminster CA

Happy Fathers Day Ike Warehime of Santee CA! You have always been one of my biggest supporters with everything I've done from all my traveling with soccer and softball to now racing quads. I love you very much!! - Kera Berry, El Cajon CA

Three Generations of off roaders in the desert. Mark Hutchins - Papa (Grandpa), CJ Hutchins - Dad and Christian Hutchins - Son/Grandson. Passing down their love of everything off road and FAST!!!!
- Journee Richardson, Henderson NV

Playing in the snow. Jesse McPheeters with his girls, Ashlynn, Sadie, and Lilah at McCain Valley. Jan '21. Photo by Papa Doug, Santee CA

Mercedes and dad Steve Lordigyan from Lakeside CA

Here's me with my Dad at the track in Carlsbad, 1974 - Bill Quackenbush, San Diego CA

Off road dads and family - Keith Lewis, Alpine CA

OFF ROAD DADS

My son Ed and I celebrating Earth Day. I just thought blowing two-stroke smoke was a great way to celebrate Earth Day. I'm OHV positive. - Vinnie Barbarino, Buena Park CA

Kevin Conrad, Dean Jarvis, Dean Jarvis Jr and the youngest in the front is Alex Jarvis.

My distant cousin and one of my best friends, Dean Jarvis, who hails from Henderson, Nevada, is not only an incredible individual but also an ardent supporter and participant in the off-roading community.

Dean's passion for off-roading is evident in how he encourages his sons, Kevin, Dean Jr., and Alex, as well as his nephew, Jason Jr., to participate in motorcycle, ATV, and UTV riding. He believes that these activities not only provide a thrilling experience but also foster a strong bond among family members.

In my pursuit of off-roading, Dean has been a constant source of support and encouragement. He has shared invaluable advice and guidance, helping me to hone my skills and become a better rider. Moreover, his enthusiasm for the sport has

been contagious, inspiring me to push my limits and explore new terrains.

Dean's dedication to off-roading extends beyond his family, as he is always eager to teach and assist others in the community. He ensures that all the "toys" are running smoothly and safely, meticulously maintaining and repairing them as needed. Dean's expertise and willingness to help have made him an instrumental figure in our off-roading circle.

I am incredibly grateful to have Dean as both a cousin and a friend. His unwavering support and passion for off-roading have made a lasting impact on my life and the lives of those around him. I hope that by sharing his story, I can inspire others to embrace the thrilling world of off-roading and foster a sense of camaraderie among fellow enthusiasts.
- David Sanders, Henderson NV

A great husband, veteran, friend and dad! Matt Myres is an off-road champion: 2011 and 2013 in the heavy metal class with VORRA and in the UTV Pro/NA class with our son Cade in 2020. His blood flowing passion for off-road has aided in his recovery of a major life changing injury in 2011. He continues to impress with his tenacity and passion for life and his ability to be a machine! Still currently racing, our son and daughter have both been in the car and Matt has supported them every step of the way. We are currently first in points for our Pro/NA UTV class and we are excited to see how this year finishes up! I'm excited to be the other driver on our family team and thank you for everything you have given our amazing family! Happy Fathers Day! - Debbie Myres, Reno Nevada

Dad Ryan Leonard, and sons Caleb, Caden and Ty

Virginia City

April 29-30, 2023
Virginia City NV
www.vcgp.com
Photos by Jeff Waldaias Photos

This year's running of the Virginia City Grand Prix saw a total of 776 racers compete on the 21 mile course over two days. Saturday's Pro/Expert/Amateur race was a 4-hour race to finish, and Sunday's Novice/Vintage/Diva/etc race was a 3-hour race to finish. There was also a mini bike race that had 55 racers in it between Minis (65s) and PeeWees (50s).

"The VCGP is always a great weekend! Such an amazing atmosphere with thousands of people coming into town for the race and a weekend full of great stories, laughs, and memories to be made. This year was one of the most fun courses I've had the chance to race on. Even though the Comstock won this year I'll be back again and again. Thank you to the VCMC and Michael's Reno Powersports for putting on another awesome race weekend!"
- Bram DeMartile

Open Pro racers: #4 Tanner Jacobson, #5 Zane Roberts finished first overall on Saturday and #3 Russell Tojum finished sixth overall also on Saturday

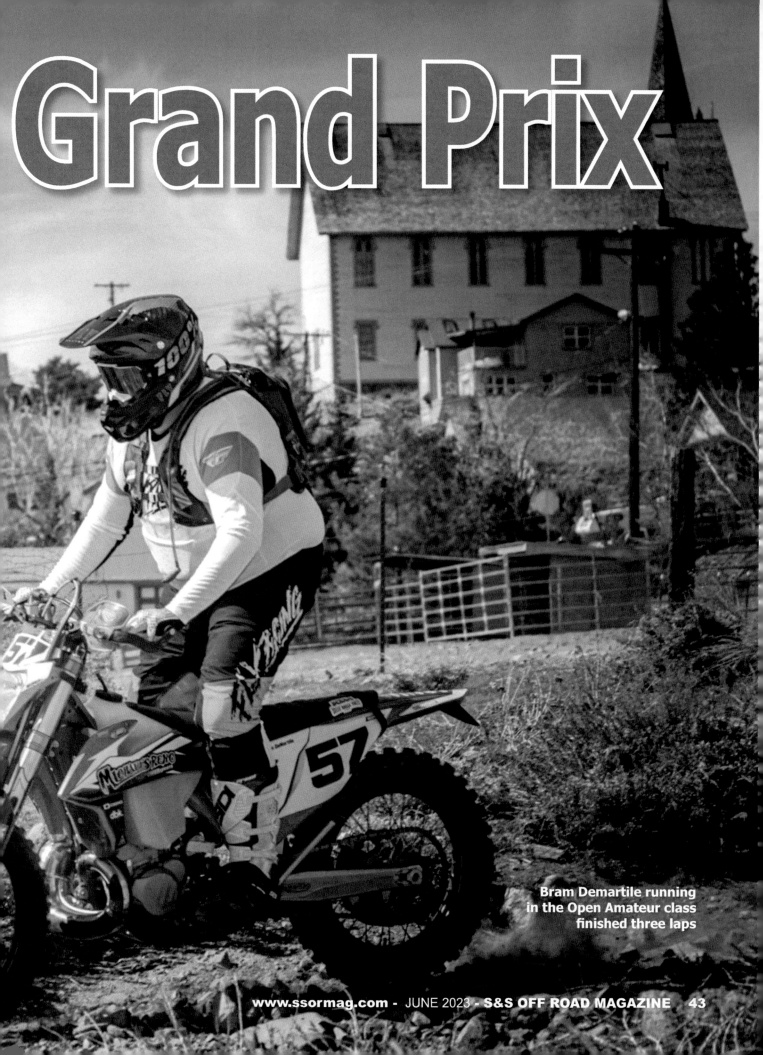

Grand Prix

Bram Demartile running
in the Open Amateur class
finished three laps

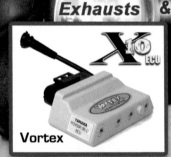

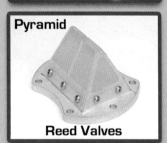

An iconic event 52 years in the making

From the Virginia City Grand Prix website

The Virginia City Grand Prix was first run in 1971, founded by Western State Racing Association (WSRA) as an AMA sanctioned event. The race quickly gained notoriety within the racing community, with its challenging course and the unique setting in the historic landmark town that flourished in the mid-1800's as mining exploded across the Comstock Load, one of the richest silver and gold resources ever discovered.

For 30 years WSRA hosted the event and welcomed many legendary competitors, including Larry Roeseler, Ty Davis, Danny Hamel, Carl Cranke and Shane Esposito. In the year 2000, WSRA hosted it's 30th and final VCGP, complete with "RIP" tombstone-shaped finishers awards to mark the end of their run.

In 2001, the tourism and special events-driven town quickly felt the loss of a major annual event and sought to address the void. In 2002, the Virginia City Motorcycle Club was formed and the VCGP was once again in action on the Comstock, this time as part of the desert racing series MRANN (Motorcycle Racing Association of Northern Nevada). After 3 years as an MRANN event, the VCGP went "outlaw" and has since been unaffiliated with any sanctioning race organization, contributing further to the event's unique character and its dedicated following by racers and fans throughout the years.

Today, the Virginia City Motorsports Club is proud to continue the tradition by hosting the VCGP. Racers and fans find that nothing compares to this challenging race through the rugged terrain surrounding Virginia City, with the unique setting of an authentic old west mining town and the amazing energy generated by this multi-day event.

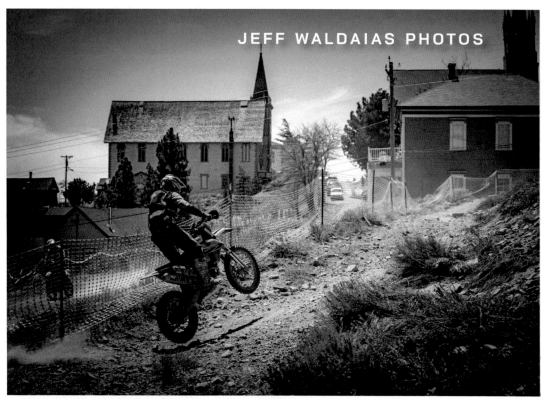

JEFF WALDAIAS PHOTOS

Keith Lovejoy, sixth Open Expert on Saturday

#158 Jacob Jones running in the 30+ Amateur class finished three laps and #161 Andrew Webber, fourth 50+ Expert

Josh Preston out of Oregon City OR finished 23rd 40+ Amateur on Sunday

OVERALL SATURDAY: 1. Zane Roberts (BET) 2. Austin Serpa 3. Ross Neely 4. Jt Baker 5. Corey Fletcher 6. Russell Tonjum (HON) 7. Red Herrera (GG) 8. Josh Cook (HUS) 9. Grayson Pringle (YAM) 10. Bronson Lee

OVERALL SUNDAY: 1. Robert Dawson (YAM) 2. Titan Allen (KTM) 3. Joshua Hoyt (HUS) 4. Colten Leavitt 5. Mikael Millan 6. Wyatt Rankin (YAM) 7. Tim Paul (KTM) 8. Mike Selkow 9. Aiden Diaz (BET) 10. Doug Mckellar

OVERALL PEEWEE: 1. Ducati Fayet (KTM) 2. Mason Heiner (KTM) 2. Mason Heiner (KTM) 3. Emmett Clark (HUS) 4. Caleb Salaices (KTM) 5. Wade Lavezzo (GG) 6. Levi Loer (HUS) 7. Stetson Starr (KTM) 8. Tanner Hatfield (HUS) 9. Taytum Main (KTM) 10. Austin Van Gorder (KTM)

OVERALL MINI: 1. Wade Clark (YAM) 2. Maverick Parke (GG) 3. Vanghn Brannan 4. Wyatt Mirell (KTM) 5. Cash Austin (HON) 6. Duke Arbogast (KTM) 7. Parker Hatfield (HUS) 8. Mason Heiner (KTM) 9. Weston Starr (KTM) 10. Ducati Fayet (KTM)

OPEN PRO: 1. Zane Roberts (BET) 2. Austin Serpa 3. Ross Neely 4. Jt Baker 5. Corey Fletcher

VET PRO: 1. Red Herrera (GG) 2. Josh Cook (HUS) 3. Sean Berryman 4. James Mcmurray (KTM) 5. Corin Fator

125 EXP: 1. Gregory Pheasant (HON)

250 EXP: 1. Bronson Lee 2. Carson Burns (KTM) 3. Austin Wilson 4. Ricky Dahlberg (YAM) 5. Dawson Working

OPEN EXP: 1. Jared Snetsinger 2. Jason Snetsinger (KTM) 3. James Yarnell 4. Bradley Hall 5. Colton Ascariz (KTM)

30+ EXP: 1. Austin Sanguinetti (KTM) 2. Matt Rhoades (HUS) 3. Weston Furia (HUS) 4. Nathaniel Mendoza (KTM) 5. Nick Cusato

40+ EXP: 1. Stu Soars (KTM) 2. Jason Andrews (KAW) 3. Woody Evens 4. Paul Bergstrom (HUS) 5. Kristofer Kierce

50+ EXP: 1. Paul Working 2. Mark Fitzsimmons (GG) 3. Kevin Yarnell 4. Andrew Webber 5. Mike Cullen (YAM)

60+ EXP: 1. Alan Myler (BRG) 2. Richard Ramsay 3. Charles Coleman (GG)

WOM EXP: 1. Nichole Collins (KTM) 2. Christina Courtney (GG) 3. Dominique Fort (KTM) 4. Heather Salaices (KTM) 5. Darcy Johnson (HUS)

125 AM: 1. Benjamin Malone

250 AM: 1. Blair Rankin (YAM) 2. Nathan Cope 3. Clayton Sheard (YAM) 4. Ollie Bonner (YAM) 5. Danny Traylor (KTM)

OPEN AM: 1. Harrison Shannon 2. Antony Vandover 3. Daniel Kough 4. Ash Rodrigues (KTM) 5. Joseph Holzer

30+ AM: 1. Tim Sleeper (KTM) 2. Robert Miles 3. Cody Fodrini 4. Joey Lasiter (KAW) 5. John Hall (KAW)

40+ AM: 1. Joshua Hoyt (HUS) 2. James Badia (BET) 3. James Shoemate 4. Marshall Bellm (HUS) 5. Tom Sheard (YAM)

50+ AM: 1. Michael Steyer (HUS) 2. Rj Moore (YAM) 3. Joseph Smith (KTM) 4. Jason Mascari (HON) 5. Chris Martin (BET)

JEFF WALDAIAS PHOTOS

#189 David Garrett finished 17th Open Amateur followed by #360 Joseph Carmo in 18th on Saturday at the Virginia City Grand Prix

WARR AM/EXP: 1. Westen Rogers (KTM) 2. Ed Canadas (KTM) 3. Jesse Cunnally (KTM) 4. Jordan Guess (KTM) 5. Aj Brumit-Salaices

125 NOV: 1. Titan Allen (KTM) 2. Colten Leavitt 3. Dustin Danen (HUS) 4. Jake Bohan 5. Gatlin Knight (HUS)

250 NOV: 1. Wyatt Rankin (YAM) 2. Aiden Diaz (BET) 3. Troy Burk (KTM) 4. Grant Gomes (KTM) 5. Ryan Downing (KTM)

OPEN NOV: 1. Robert Dawson (YAM) 2. Joshua Hoyt (HUS) 3. Mike Selkow 4. Michael Venezia 5. Quinn Holzer (HON)

30+ NOV: 1. Mikael Millan 2. Blake Hoffmann (KTM) 3. Taylor Tobler 4. Johnathan Ayers 5. Matt Mrizek

40+ NOV: 1. Tim Paul (KTM) 2. Doug Mckellar 3. Jason Behm (HUS) 4. Jeremy Rosenbach (YAM) 5. Cain Fisher (KTM)

50+ NOV: 1. Shane Smith (KTM) 2. Aaron Burns 3. Jerry Schumann (KAW) 4. Bradley Moore (YAM) 5. Craig Ingersoll (KTM)

WARR NOV: 1. Jacob Roseberry 2. Scott Stites (YAM) 3. Colton Hults (KTM) 4. Jamie Hamon (KTM) 5. James Ridlen

BOMB AM/NOV: 1. Ryan Jackson 2. Steve Walkiewicz 3. Lochlan Campbell (KAW) 4. Adam Devargas

WOM AM/NOV: 1. Rachel Roen (YAM) 2. Kylah Krupa (KTM) 3. Robyn Embrey (BET) 4. Chelsea Rust 5. Taylor Kemp (YAM)

MAS 60-69: 1. Bob Baron (HUS) 2. Rocky Tilander (HUS) 3. Mark Conrad (YAM) 4. Dave Florez 5. Thomas Jensen (HUS)

ULTRA MAS 70+: 1. Daniel Stipkovich (KTM) 2. Danny Bawdon (HUS) 3. Larry Cunnally (KTM)

VINTAGE: 1. Donn Williams 2. Jason Shakespeare 3. Mike Johnson 4. Tom Maples (SUZ) 5. Chris Brady (HUS)

ADVENTURE: 1. Nicholas Breshears

DIVA: 1. Alexus Vaughn 2. Siarra Whitmore (KTM) 3. Britan Canadas 4. Karen Sked (BET) 5. Jen Burns

D SPORT NOV: 1. Daniel Hall (KTM) 2. Lance Coleman (HUS)

ELECTRIC: 1. Merlin Valencia

MINI EXP: 1. Vanghn Brannan 2. Wyatt Mirell (KTM) 3. Cash Austin (HON)

MINI AM: 1. Wade Clark (YAM) 2. Maverick Parke (GG) 3. Duke Arbogast (KTM) 4. Parker Hatfield (HUS) 5. Ducati Fayet (KTM)

MINI NOV: 1. Mason Heiner (KTM) 2. Weston Starr (KTM) 3. Tucker Jones 4. Hunter Welton 5. Payslee Starr (KTM)

PW 7-9: 1. Ducati Fayet (KTM) 2. Mason Heiner (KTM) 3. Emmett Clark (HUS) 4. Caleb Salaices (KTM) 5. Levi Loer (HUS)

PW 4-6: 1. Wade Lavezzo (GG) 2. Tanner Hatfield (HUS) 3. Bria Lasiter (HUS) 4. Lane Rodriguez (HON) 5. Waylon Dempsey 🔋

JEFF WALDAIAS PHOTOS

Chris Bartkowski, 18th 30+ Amateur

New Club Logo!

AMA NATIONAL DUAL SPORT SERIES

29th Annual **BIG BEAR RUN**

JUNE 24th & 25th, 2023

A two day Dual Sport Motorcycle tour of the mountains surrounding Big Bear Lake. Finisher plaques will be awarded to those who complete Saturday's hard loop. All skill levels are welcome. Saturday will have easy/hard options, and *adventure bike* routes to choose from. GPS Data available at sign up (bring your own GPS, and data cable), _NO_ **roll charts**

MEMBERSHIP REQUIRED

Join AMA: AmericanMotorcyclist.com

SIGN-UPS & BANQUET WILL BE HELD AT:

BEAR MOUNTAIN RESORT 43101 GOLDMINE DR. BIG BEAR LAKE, CA 92315

REGISTRATION OPENS
Friday: 3pm to 10pm
Saturday: 6am to 9am

Sign-Up online BigBearTrailRiders.com

LARGE VENDOR ROW
Featuring lots of new products & information!

- Overnight RV parking permit will be available at the Bear Mountain Resort parking lot at a low cost of $25 per vehicle. This parking permit option will be available on the BBTR website registration page for purchase to reserve your spot. You will need to bring a print out and present your proof of purchase to parking attendant when you arrive to enter overnight parking lot reserved area. No hook-ups.
- Parking lot will be open at 12pm Friday For RV & day use parking with restroom facilities open until 10pm everyday.
- Day use parking area is free of charge.
- Saturday rider entry includes Saturday night Banquet with great sponsor giveaways.
- Paid Pre-entry guarantees an event T-Shirt.

Street Legal / Licensed motorcycles only. Spark arrestor mandatory.
For information call Jim Nicholson (818) 391-3083, Frank Schnetz (909) 225-7409 or Miguel Burgi (818) 391-3031

Follow Us On

TEAR DOWN TIME

Rich Stevens
putting in a clutch
in the Suzuki
Samurai
- Susan Stephens,
Ocotillo Wells CA

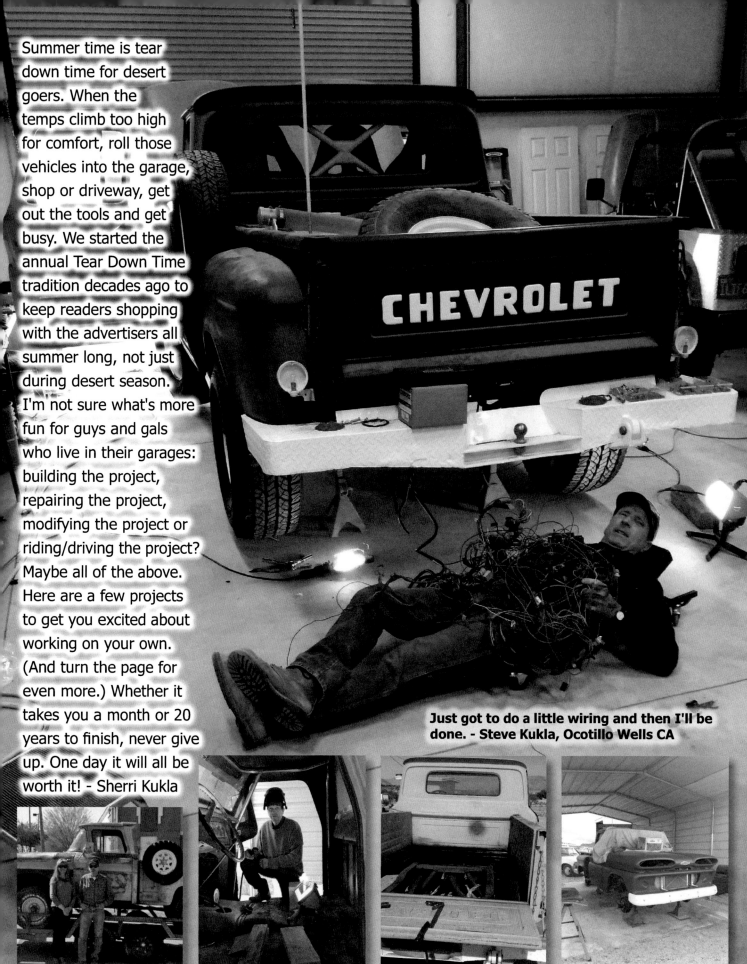

Summer time is tear down time for desert goers. When the temps climb too high for comfort, roll those vehicles into the garage, shop or driveway, get out the tools and get busy. We started the annual Tear Down Time tradition decades ago to keep readers shopping with the advertisers all summer long, not just during desert season. I'm not sure what's more fun for guys and gals who live in their garages: building the project, repairing the project, modifying the project or riding/driving the project? Maybe all of the above. Here are a few projects to get you excited about working on your own. (And turn the page for even more.) Whether it takes you a month or 20 years to finish, never give up. One day it will all be worth it! - Sherri Kukla

Just got to do a little wiring and then I'll be done. - Steve Kukla, Ocotillo Wells CA

TEAR DOWN TIME

Slowly getting my other quad up and running to be either the race bike or desert bike. - Kera Berry, El Cajon CA

Race Schedule 2023

4WP DESERT SHOWDOWN
January 25-29, 2023
Pahrump, NV

VT Construction Battleground
March 23-26, 2023
Caliente, NV

Baja Nevada
May 10-13 2023
Nevada

UTV Freedom Ride
June 23-25, 2023
Location TBD

Dirt Rebelution
September 22-24, 2023
Cedar City, UT

Gold Rush
October 19-22, 2023
Virginia City to Tonopah, NV

Stateline Shootout
November 30, December 1-3, 2023
Primm, NV

TEAR DOWN TIME

This is my latest project which I have been working on for the past few months. I found this 1975 Honda ST90 baking in the Arizona desert sun and bought it for $300.

It was missing a few parts and the headlight had melted due to a wiring short.

These ST90's (which were only made for 3 years) were 90cc and had 3 speed motors. I installed a low miles 1985 Honda ATC 125 4 speed motor with electric and pull start. I added a 24mm Mikuni flat slide carb and built the exhaust with an old style Supertrapp spark arrestor to keep it forest and desert legal. Suspension was upgraded with Kawasaki KLX140 forks (with disc brake). I also adapted a longer swingarm and mid 1970's Boge rear shocks. There are many hand made parts and modifications on this little bike all done in my garage workshop.

I avoided the cheap China Honda clone parts that currently flood the marketplace.

Except for the forks and front brake, it has for the most part been built out of Japanese parts from my junk pile. My friend has dubbed it the "Mutt Dawg." The bike rides real nice off road and is street licensed.

As a test of it's viability I entered it in the Biltwell 100 Desert Race on April 1st in the Misfit class and came in first place in the pull start division and second overall in the open Misfit class.

It was a fun low budget build which shows you don't need to spend 10-20K to have fun off road.

- Randy Ressell, Lifetime S&S Off Road Magazine subscriber, Orange County CA

Got the Negrete 5-1600 back in my shop after the Mint 400. Getting ready for the upcoming Record Night Race Ensenada to San Felipe June 24 - Dave Simpson, Corona CA

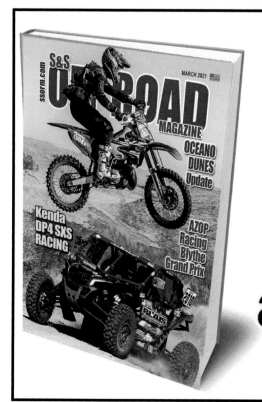
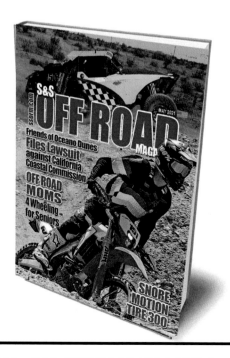

Single seater GSXR1300 with a reverser box. Sequential shift, power steering, tilt wheel, heated seat.
- Mark Patenaude, Santee CA

Richard Calahan of Temecula prepping the Bronco for next season in Ocotillo Wells. 🧑‍🔧

From the AMA Motorcycle Hall of Fame

Ron Bishop

This Baja legend raced every Baja 1000 from 1967 to 2012 in addition to Baja 500s, Tecate 500 Enduros, and two ISDTs. Dealer in Escondido until his passing

Ron Bishop in 2002

Ron Bishop became a legend in long distance off-road races such as the famous Baja 1000. Bishop raced every Baja 1000 from its start in 1967 to the time he was inducted into the Motorcycle Hall of Fame in 2001 and beyond. He won numerous class titles in many of the major off-road motorcycle races of the 1960s through the early 2000s, such as the Baja 1000, Baja 500, Tecate 500, Mint 400 and Mexicale 300.

During the mid-1970s Bishop was also a two-time

member of the American team in the International Six-Day Trials (ISDT, now called ISDE). Bishop was a factory off-road racer for Kawasaki and later Rokon.

Bishop was born in Woodland, Washington, in March of 1943. His family moved to Southern California when he was 10 and settled in Escondido. The area was a hotbed of off-road motorcycling and most of Bishop's friends had motorcycles. Bishop's first ride was a Cushman Eagle scooter, which he naturally took off-road. He rapidly moved from the scooter to a Mustang and eventually to what Bishop called his first real motorcycle — a Zundapp 250cc Super Sabre.

In 1960, Bishop began racing scrambles and TT races.

"I'd race a TT every Friday night at Cajon Speedway in El Cajon," Bishop recalled. "Then I'd put knobbies on the bike and go scrambles racing that weekend."

Bishop learned from watching some of the San Diego area's top riders, such as Cal Rayborn and Ralph White. While Bishop enjoyed racing TT and scrambles, he found the waiting around between races to be excruciating.

"You'd race then sit around for hours until you got to race again," Bishop remembers. But in enduros, hare scrambles and long-distance desert races, Bishop found his calling. In those events, there was no waiting around, just hours of wide-open racing.

Bishop rode many of the major off-road races of his era. The Greenhorn Enduro, Barstow to Vegas and the grueling long-distance races such as the Mint 400 and the Baja 1000. Bishop became one of the leading off-road racers on the West Coast, but he wanted to prove himself among the best in the country. In the early-to-mid-1970s, the opportunity to show his skills outside of the West came in the form of ISDT qualifiers held throughout the country. Bishop earned a factory Kawasaki ride in 1973. It was a plush life by the normally low-dollar standards of off-road racers. Bishop flew to the races, stayed in nice hotels and had mechanics looking after his motorcycles. Off-road racing legend Walt Axthelm was the team's manager.

Bishop, who grew up on the hard-packed, dusty and wide-open trails of Southern California, learned to ride in

www.SCFTARacing.com

SCFTA
SOUTHERN CALIFORNIA FLAT TRACK ASSOCIATION

SOUTHERN
CALIFORNIA'S
PREMIER
FLAT
TRACK
FACILITY

Photo: Hangar 53 Studio

@SCFTARacing

Saturday, June 3
Gates Open @ 12 pm | Riders Meeting @ 2:45 pm
Practice @ 3 pm | Racing to follow...
Sunday, June 4
Gates Open @ 8 am Riders Meeting @ 9:45 pm
Practice @ 10 am | Racing to follow...

1205 Burton Road - Perris, CA 92570 USA www.**scftaracing**.com

KIDS RACE FREE
YOUTH 50cc - 65cc entry fees are FREE
Sponsored by Rod Lake Racing

2023
JUNE 3 & 4 - **Rounds 5 & 6**
JULY - AUGUST Dark No Racing
SEPTEMBER 16 - **Round 7**
OCTOBER 7 - **Round 8**
NOVEMBER 11 & 12 - **Rounds 9 & 10**
DECEMBER 9 - **Round 11** (double points)

the tight trees, loamy dirt and often muddy conditions of the East Coast races, making him one of the most versatile off-roaders of his era.

He qualified for the 1973 ISDT, held in the United States for the first time in the scenic Berkshire Mountains in western Massachusetts. Unfortunately, Bishop's, and the other factory Kawasakis, all experienced gearbox failures in the international competition and he did not finish the race.

Even though his first ISDT outing wasn't a success on the track, Bishop still very much enjoyed the experience. He came back and qualified again for the ISDT in 1975, riding for the factory Rokon squad. That year, the prestigious weeklong event was held on the Isle of Man. Halfway through that year's race, Bishop suffered a hard crash and broke ribs, once again putting him out of the race. Nevertheless, Bishop later said representing his country in two ISDT appearances was among the most memorable episodes of his racing career.

Being a factory Rokon rider gave Bishop a great insight on one of the most unique off-road racing motorcycles in the history of the sport. Rokons featured automatic

transmissions. Bishop recalls the special riding techniques it took to ride this unusual bike.

"The Rokon would freewheel down hills so you had to go against your instincts and give it throttle to actually control the back end of the bike," Bishop said. "It had a snowmobile-style drive. One good thing about it was you couldn't kill the engine. If you fell off the thing it would just lie there and idle. Going up hills if the rear tire started to break loose it would just gear up until it quit spinning. It was a great concept, but it was probably 60 pounds heavier than other bikes of that era and that extra weight would wear on you."

The Baja 1000 first ran in 1967 and quickly became one of the best-known off-road races in the world. Over the years, Bishop became a legend in the race for competing in every Baja 1000 from its start in 1967 through the early 2000s. His best result in the race was overall runner-up in 1972 with co-rider Don Bohannon. The two of them rode a highly modified Suzuki TM400.

"In the early days of Baja it was just you and a co-rider," Bishop explains as he shows a photo of him in an

early race wearing a military canteen, black leather riding pants and lineman boots. "The event has become so complex that in the 2001 race our team consisted of 37 crew members and 13 support vehicles, along with all the GPS systems and high-tech communications gear. It's really something."

By the 2000s, the average speed of the race nearly doubled from the time Bishop first raced Baja in the 1960s.

Bishop described in vivid detail the tricks your mind would play on you after 14 hours on the bike riding at night. "You would start to hallucinate from fatigue," he said. "Cactus looked like they were moving and you began hoping that the boulders, which started looking like houses, were the final checkpoint."

During his years of off-road racing, Bishop became a self-taught electrical engineer of sorts and began developing more powerful lighting for his motorcycles. He was the first to figure out how to power halogen lights on his bikes. He earned such a reputation for his electrical and lighting systems that he worked for several factories over the years supplying them with bright and reliable lighting for high-speed racing in the dark desert.

In the early 1980s, Bishop opened his own motorcycle shop, dealing exclusively in off-road motorcycles. Through his shop, Bishop worked with many of the leading off-road and motocross riders of the greater San Diego area from the 1980s to 2014.

Mr. Bishop was inducted into the AMA Motorcycle Hall of Fame in 2001. He passed away in September 2014.

Reprinted with permission from the American Motorcyclist Association, home of the AMA's re-imagined and re-engineered *American Motorcyclist* magazine, North America's largest-circulation and best multi-discipline motorcycle enthusiast publication. *American Motorcyclist* covers it all, from amateur and professional racing to events, rights issues and motorcycle history, and everything in between, including a monthly column by HOFer Malcolm Smith. Become an AMA member and get *American Motorcyclist* delivered to your door every month for just $4.08 per month. To learn more: www.Americanmotorcyclist.com

SCFTA FLAT TRACK

April 15, 2023 - Round 4
Perris Raceway, Perris CA
www.scftaracing.com
Photos by Lady Jane

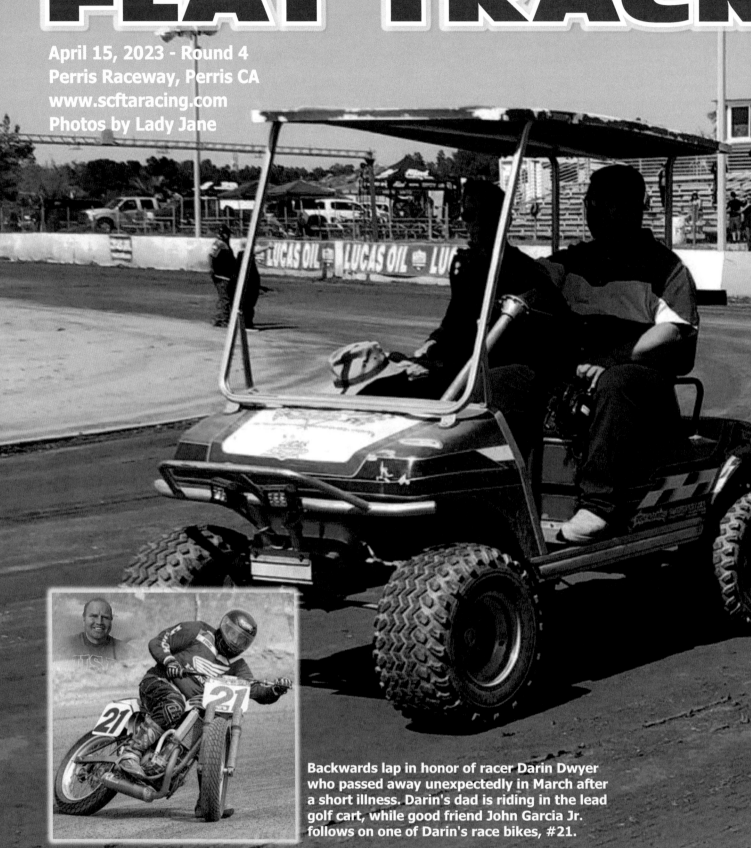

Backwards lap in honor of racer Darin Dwyer who passed away unexpectedly in March after a short illness. Darin's dad is riding in the lead golf cart, while good friend John Garcia Jr. follows on one of Darin's race bikes, #21.

#71M Jon Nunes, first Vet +35 Expert followed by #23 Nick Garcia who finished in third, Adam Lesley moved into second place and #48 Dan Brown finished fourth

RESULTS

50cc 2 Stk Beg 1. Rey Resendez 2. Isla Ferris 3. Bowen Eikelberger

50cc 2 Stk Nov 1. Thomas Chavira 2. Ben Eikelberger 3. Bryce Eikelberger

50cc 2 Stk Am 1. Travis Vick

50cc Open 1. Thomas Chavira 2. Ben Eikelberger 3. Isla Ferris 4. Bryce Eikelberger

65cc 2 Stk Beg 1. Thomas Chavira 2. Ben Eikelberger 3. Rey Resendez 4. Bryce Eikelberger

85cc 2 Stk Beg 1. Dylan Pederson

65cc Open 1. Thomas Chavira 2. Bryce Eikelberger 3. Ben Eikelberger

80 Open 1. Dylan Pedersen

Bomber Exp 1. Joe Steffen 2. Robbie Crean 3. Brandon Gerdes 4. Don Jensen

Bomber Am 1. Paul Claybaugh 2. Dwayne Locke

Vet +50 Exp 1. Jon Nunes 2. Matt Stoutenburg 3. Bill Kolkman 4. Adam Lesley 5. Jeff Apple

Vet +50 Am/Nov 1. Gene Brown 2. Keith Guthery 3. Billy Beck 4. Jerry Schennamsgruber

Madd Dog 1. Evin Perrault 2. Marc Heathfield 3. Brandi Beck 4. Mike Stepak

Classic Vintage 1. Gary Leopold 2. Joe Pape 3. Conner Hickerson 4. Bruce Gajjar 5. Lenny Rodriquez

35+ Vet Exp 1. Jon Nunes 2. Adam Lesley 3. Nick Garcia 4. Dan Brown 5. Shawn Chamlee

35+ Vet Am/Nov 1. Josh Sleigh 2. Rich Silva 3. Douglas Darrah 4. Jordan Rogers 5. TJ Bisch

Madd Dog Open 1. Conner Hickerson 2. Jasper Heathfield

Powder Puff 1. Marissa Silva 2. Brandi Beck

Vintage All 1. Bruce Gajjar 2. Chris Roysdon 3. Dwayne Locke

Open Exp 1. Travis Petton 2. Matt Stoutenburg 3. Colin Petton 4. Conner Hickerson 5. Joshua Lesley

Sup Sen Exp 1. Joe Steffen 2. Bill Kolkman 3. James Morris 4. Elliott Iverson 5. Johnny Custom

Open Nov/Beg 1. Jasper Heathfield 2. Brandi Beck 3. Chris Piccirillo

Open Am 1. Billy Beck 2. TJ Bisch 3. Summer Kukla 4. Dan Brown

Open Unclassified 1. Colin Petton 2. Joshua Lesley

Framer Exp 1. James Morris 2. Adam Lesley 3. Johnny Custom 4. Brandon Gerdes

Framer Am/Nov 1. Terry Williams 2. Joey Crabtree 3. Marissa Silva 4. Patrick Hayes

Super Sen +60 Am/Nov 1. Gene Brown 2. Terry Williams 3. Paul Claybaugh 4. Billy Beck 5. Dave Berg

Pull Starts 1. Conner Hickerson 2. Brett Miller 3. Nathan Baumgardner 4. Dylan Pedersen 5. Jake Espinoza

Hooligans 1. Adam Lesley 2. Josh Sleigh 3. Shawn Chamlee 4. Rich Silva 5. Mike Stepak

Pro 1. Travis Petton 2. Kayl Kolkman

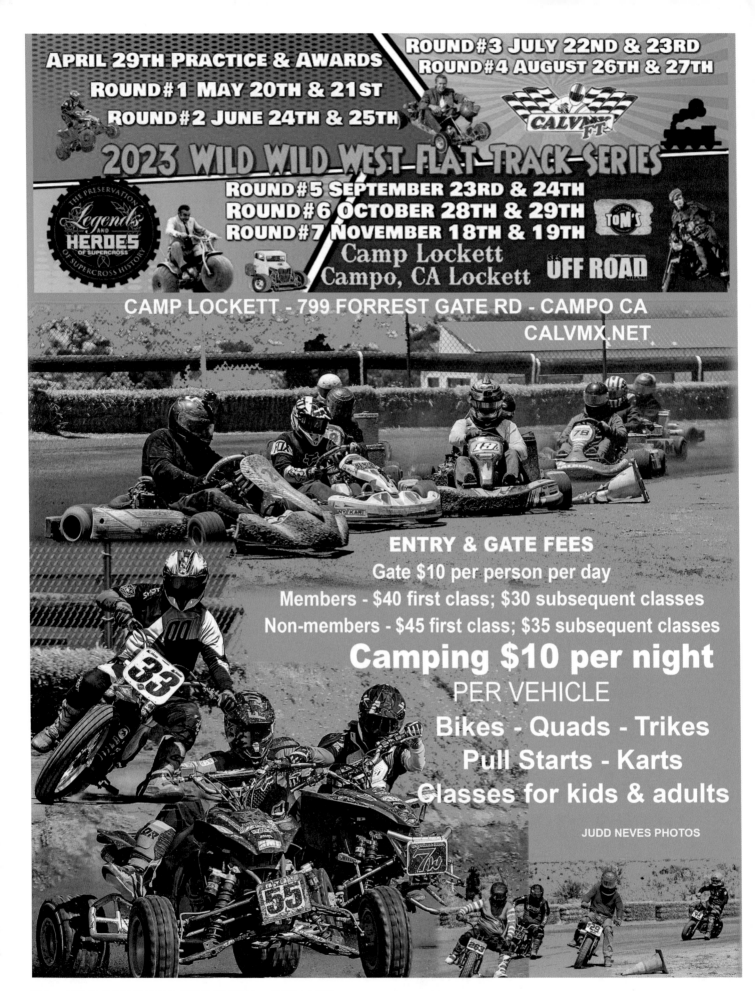

APRIL 29TH PRACTICE & AWARDS
ROUND #1 MAY 20TH & 21ST
ROUND #2 JUNE 24TH & 25TH

ROUND #3 JULY 22ND & 23RD
ROUND #4 AUGUST 26TH & 27TH

CALVMX FT

2023 WILD WILD WEST FLAT TRACK SERIES

ROUND #5 SEPTEMBER 23RD & 24TH
ROUND #6 OCTOBER 28TH & 29TH
ROUND #7 NOVEMBER 18TH & 19TH

Legends AND HEROES OF SUPERCROSS — THE PRESERVATION OF SUPERCROSS HISTORY

TOM'S

Camp Lockett
Campo, CA Lockett

S&S OFF ROAD

CAMP LOCKETT - 799 FORREST GATE RD - CAMPO CA
CALVMX.NET

ENTRY & GATE FEES
Gate $10 per person per day
Members - $40 first class; $30 subsequent classes
Non-members - $45 first class; $35 subsequent classes

Camping $10 per night
PER VEHICLE
Bikes - Quads - Trikes
Pull Starts - Karts
Classes for kids & adults

JUDD NEVES PHOTOS

#38 Shawn Chamlee, fifth 35+ Vet Expert

LADY JANE PHOTO

Only two pro racers ran in this class for Round 4, but put on a show as they battled for the lead. #82 Travis Petton finished first followed by #98 Kayl Kolkman.

BLAST FROM THE PAST

Unknown riders on these two pages captured at the 1972 Baja 500 by Trackside Photo and sent to us by the late Jim Ober. These photos originally appeared in the Blast from the Past column in our May 2016 issue.

TRACKSIDE PHOTO - www.tracksidephoto.com
In Memory of Jim Ober - Photos reprinted from previous years' Blast from the Past

BLAST FROM THE PAST CONTINUED

Norm Johnson of Las Vegas, Nevada, gets stuck in a ditch at the 1976 Baja 1000. Photo courtesy of Trackside Photo and originally appeared in the December 2015 issue

TRACKSIDE PHOTO.COM

Ben and Mike Hibbs from San Diego at the 1986 High Desert Racing 250 at Barstow. Mike Julson was also a co-driver. Originally printed in the July 2016 Blast from the Past column.

ABOVE 59th Annual Lakeside Rodeo Western Days Parade RIGHT Corral Canyon OHV Trail Work 5.6.23 Lots of Growth - Lots of work still needs to be done. Fallen trees on the trail. Over growth. Spring time blooms. Water falls and creek crossings. What a gorgeous day working on the trail.

San Diego Off-Road Coalition

THE ENDANGERED OFF ROADER

OFFICIAL NEWSLETTER BY SDORC PRESIDENT ED STOVIN WWW.SDORC.ORG

Jamboree

SDORC is having an Off-Road Jamboree this June 24th at Lakeside Rodeo Grounds in Lakeside CA. So far we have 42 vendors signed up, 8 nonprofits and clubs, several race team vehicles and drivers (with a trophy truck), a top fuel dragster and RC car racing in the arena (bring your own car!). There will be a large raffle at 5:00 pm (think Lost Lizard raffle) that is chock full of cool off-road stuff. Chris Boyer will be our MC. There will be food trucks and beverages. $20 will get you in the door and $40 will get you in with a special BBQ dinner. Go to https://sdorc.org/jamboree/ to get details and sign up early. This is a big fundraiser for SDORC so we can hire a top flight lobbyist to help keep the desert open. The event is designed to be loads of fun, so please save the day for us.

Mojave Trails National Monument

The BLM is forming a management plan for the MTNM. I was appointed to the advisory committee and took several tours of the area. They are starting the management plan with a phase called scoping. At scoping we can tell the BLM how we would like the plan formed and what topics included. We intend to ask for a number of items including: continuing to allow organized events, allow commercial activities (like movie filming), continue to allow rock hounding (where people look for interesting minerals), protect certain WWII areas and artifacts (General Patton had extensive training in this area) and keep trails open for off-road vehicle use. If you are interested, you can find details here:

https://www.federalregister.gov/documents/2023/05/05/2023-09619/notice-of-intent-to-amend-the-california-desert-conservation-area-plan-associated-with-the-mojave

BLM Conservation

Our friends at Blue Ribbon Coalition told us that the BLM is proposing a national rule change that would elevate conservation to be part of "multiple use." From the BLM: "FLPMA's declaration of policy and definitions of 'multiple use' and 'sustained yield' reveal that conservation is a use on par with other uses under FLPMA." FLPMA is Federal Land Policy and Management Act. The BLM would be allowed to sell "conservation leases" on public land. This could allow groupslike the Sierra Club, to buy leases and control public land. The rule change would also make it easier to designate "Areas of Critical Environmental Concern". Public comments on this are being taken until June 20th. Details can be found at https://www.regulations.gov/document/BLM-2023-0001-0001

CARB On Road Motorcycles

CARB has come out with proposed on road motorcycle emissions standards. I wrote about this last year and they have taken the next step towards implementing updates. Comments from the public are being accepted until June 2, 2023. I haven't gotten into the document yet, but if you love dual sport motorcycles, you might want to look here https://ww2.arb.ca.gov/sites/default/files/2023-05/ONMC%20Reg%20Text_DRAFT%2005102023.pdf

Corral Canyon

We were part of a trail trimming day at Corral Canyon on May 6th. There were about 80 4X4s and two motorcycles. I took my bike over to the Greenhorn trail and trimmed the whole length. Most of the 4X4 trails were trimmed, but I hear parts of the Espinoza Trail still need work. I'd like to thank Tierra Del Sol 4x4 Club for covering the BBQ.

Grants

We look at green sticker grants each year to make sure our money is being spent wisely. Yes, there is a grant program where about $30M gets allocated each year. We look at grants in the southern half of the state. This year we didn't find much funny business (like in years past) but we did find some interesting applications. Imperial County Sheriff's Department asked for money for two big ticket vehicles, a V8 buggy ($130,000) and a 1/2 ton 4X4 truck ($110,000). I thought it was odd for them to want a V8 buggy until Audrey told me that they really need one to chase down bad guys out in the sand dunes. That made sense to me. The 4X4 made sense, until I saw the price tag. That's a lot of money for a truck. When I went to the Los Angeles County Sheriff's grant, I saw they wanted the same truck, but only asked for $50,000. I sent the LA Sheriff's contact to Imperial County and suggested they talk to them and ask how they can get the same truck for that price. Imperial County actually wrote me back saying they would contact LA County.

Yamaha

You may remember we put new rice bales around the kid's training area at Corral Canyon a few months ago. We wrote a grant request to Yamaha to help pay for the bales and we just found out Yamaha approved our request! Thank you, Yamaha, on behalf of SDORC and all the kids riding out there.

Help SDORC

Please listen to SDORC Dirt Talk Radio on 1170am on Sundays at noon or after that on our website https://sdorc.org/sdorc-radio/ Come to a meeting on the first Tuesday of each month at Ranch House Restaurant in Santee, (Bill Wells, running for congress, will be coming to speak in June) and join SDORC (we are a membership organization) at https://sdorc.org/join-sdorc/ and please come to our Jamboree on June 24th.
-Ed Stovin 🏍️

Join San Diego Off Road Coalition to help protect off road areas www.sdorc.org/join-sdorc/

CALVMX LEGENDS & HEROES VINTAGE MOTOCROSS

Perris Raceway - Perris CA
Round 1 - April 16, 2023
www.calvmx.net
By Steve Caro
Photos by Kathryn Caro

#8 Scott Burnworth with
#36X Johannes Wonrooij

CALVMX returned to the legendary Perris Raceway for the first time since before the 2020 mandated lockdown. Round one of the four-round series was held in near perfect weather conditions. The new management operating the raceway were extremely obliging as they altered the Vet Track to accommodate the older machinery that comprises vintage racing. The winding course was a perfect fit for the wide variety of machines comprising a CALVMX event. A nice cross section of machinery dating from the late 1960's on up to the most modern machinery used in the Modern Support classes gathered in the pit area.

Leading off the day was the combined GP-1 250 Experts and GP-1 500 Intermediates and Experts. In the 500 Expert class, Shaun Hamer resumed his dominating style by getting a great start to lead Chuck Lampe and Tim Harris. Hamer's lead eventually grew to roughly three seconds over Lampe and Harris. Hamer proceeded to reel off five consistent laps to take the win, with Lampe and Harris in second and third. While Hamer was leading the 500's, Robert Kong grabbed a massive holeshot and built up an insurmountable lead over the entire field of entrants on his way to having the distinction of being the first across the finish line in the new season.

The start of the second moto was a replica of the first race. Kong again rocketed away from the old-school flag start and quickly built up a multi-bike length lead over the rest of the combined class race. Behind Kong, Hamer once again led the 500 Experts, pursued by Lampe and Harris.

Both Kong and Hamer made things look easy as Kong once again was the first rider across the line and Hamer clinched his overall division win with a 1-1 score.

CALVMX member Norm Himaka and his Maico have been fixtures in the club series' for over two decades. In a change of pace, Himaka took on a new challenge by entering the GP-3 250 Expert class on a pristine 1987 Honda CR-250. Restored from what started as a rolling basket case by his lifelong friend Gary Faxon, Himaka proved adept at adjusting to the increased suspension travel and the necessity to adjust his riding style to the more modern machine. In the first moto, Himaka employed a moderate pace to take second in the Expert portion of the moto behind Robert Kong. In the second moto, Himaka, having had time to gain familiarity with his new mount, took the moto win along with the overall victory in his first post-vintage racing endeavor.

I enjoyed a good day of racing and it was great to be racing back at Perris after a few years away. The track was in great condition and ideal for close racing with a good turnout of fast guys. - Shaun Hamer

KATHRYN CARO PHOTO

Norm Himaka finished second in the GP-3 250 Expert class

The nine moto plus Ironman schedule featured a wide variety of class winners. GP-1 500 Intermediate saw Scott Mays notching 1-1 scores to take the overall win. Andrew McKeag, dressed in period correct riding gear, captured two class wins on his immaculate late 60's and early 70's Husqvarnas. McKeag topped both the Vintage 50 Plus Experts, along with taking the win in the Classic 500 Expert race.

Johannes Wonrooij was also a double class winner with overall victories in Open Age Intermediate and GP-3 250 Intermediate competition. Newcomer Chase George also took home double overall wins in Vintage Sportsman 250 Intermediate along with scoring the win in the Vintage Intermediate portion of the Ironman class. Also collecting an overall win was Women's Beginner entrant Miki McElwain who displayed fine form as she stayed right with the combined class of GP-200 and XR-75 competition.

The second round of the 2023 series is scheduled for June 11, again at the Perris Raceway facility. CALVMX will continue its tradition of offering classes for machines ranging from the short-travel vintage bikes up to modern bikes.

KATHRYN CARO PHOTOS

Chase George also took home double overall wins in Vintage Sportsman 250 and Vintage Intermediate

AMA Motorcycle Hall of Fame Announces 2023 Nominees

AMA Motorcycle Hall of Fame Glory Days Statue

The AMA Motorcycle Hall of Fame is pleased to announce the list of nominees for the Class of 2023, and that voting is now open.

The AMA Motorcycle Hall of Fame selection committees have put forward 16 nominees from eight areas of influence: Ambassadors & Industry, Design & Engineering, Dirt Track, Leadership & Rights, Motocross & Supercross, Off-Road, Road Racing and Specialty Competition.

Nominees include:

Competition:

Jim Belland (Dirt Track)

Ryan Dungey (Motocross & Supercross)

Eraldo Ferracci (Road Racing)

Barry Hawk (Off Road)

Grant Langston (Motocross & Supercross)

Brent Thompson (Dirt Track)

Ryan Young (Specialty Competition)

Non-Competition

Rita Coombs (Ambassadors & Industry)

Robert Coy (Ambassadors & Industry)

Michael Czysz (Design & Engineering)

Travis Pastrana (Ambassadors & Industry)

Rodney Roberts (Leadership & Rights)

Paul Schlegel (Ambassadors & Industry)

Rick Sieman (Leadership & Rights)

Buddy Stubbs (Ambassadors & Industry)

Barry Willey (Design & Engineering)

"The AMA Motorcycle Hall of Fame nominees for 2023 include a diverse and accomplished group of men and women who've demonstrated exceptional achievements in competition, advocacy and promotion of the sport of motorcycling," said AMA President and CEO Rob Dingman. "They have contributed significantly to the advancement of motorcycling in various areas, from excelling in dirt track, motocross and road racing competition, to advocating for motorcyclists' rights, to creating enduring events that have helped grow motorcycling, to creating innovative motorcycle designs. We're honored to recognize this year's nominees and eagerly anticipate announcing the Class of 2023 soon." ➔

DIRTBITS

Voting for the AMA Motorcycle Hall of Fame Class of 2023 is now open. Eligible voters include previous Hall of Fame inductees, members of the AMA and AMHF Boards of Directors, and members of the AMA Motorcycle Hall of Fame Category Selection Committees. AMA Life Members with at least 25 years of consecutive membership are also eligible to vote but should update their contact information to receive the latest updates and announcements pertaining to the voting process.

Voting ends Sunday, June 18 at 11:59 p.m.

Voting results will be announced soon after voting closes, and the AMA Motorcycle Hall of Fame induction ceremony will be held on Sept. 15, in Pickerington, Ohio.

To vote on this year's nominees, visit AmericanMotorcyclist.com/hall-of-fame-class-of-2023.

450SX Crown Fulfills Honda's '23 AMA SX Championship Sweep

With a main-event win Saturday evening, May 13, aboard his CRF450RWE in Salt Lake City's Rice-Eccles Stadium, Chase Sexton wrapped up the 2023 450SX Championship at the AMA Supercross series finale. This premier-class crown follows on the heels of twin 250SX titles by Sexton's Team Honda HRC colleagues, with Jett Lawrence having clinched the West Region Championship in Denver, and Hunter Lawrence having earned the East Region laurels in Nashville.

Chase Sexton takes Honda's first premier-class AMA Supercross title in 20 years

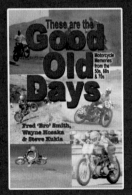

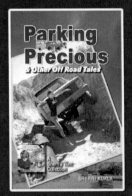

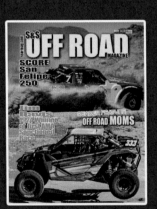

This one was particularly hard-earned, as the grueling 17-round series eliminated a number of top riders through injury. Sexton persevered, collecting six main-event wins, and he was consistently the fastest rider of all, qualifying on top at 14 of the 17 rounds. The 23-year-old set several season-best marks, including most podium finishes (13), most top-five results (16), most heat-race wins (eight) and most laps led. Of note was Sexton's upward trajectory; while his pure speed was impressive all season, he had to work hard to eliminate errors that cost him wins in the early rounds.

A native of La Moille, Illinois, Sexton is a longtime member of the Honda family, having signed with Factory Connection's amateur squad in 2015. In 2018 he transitioned to that operation's professional team, with whom he won the 250SX East Region Championship in 2019 and 2020. Sexton moved up to the factory Honda squad midyear, and he was a regular podium finisher during the 2021 season. Last year saw him earn his first AMA Supercross premier-class win, and he was victorious often outdoors, battling Eli Tomac hard throughout the series before finishing a close second in the title chase.

"Wow, 2023 450 Supercross Champion—it doesn't even feel real yet," an emotional Sexton said following the race. "It's what I've worked for since I was two-and-a-half years old, when I first got on a dirt bike; since then, this has been the goal. This year was definitely not easy; I was up-and-down in the middle of the season, but I got four of the last six wins—really came on strong at the end, when I needed to. It means so much to me. I couldn't ask for a better group of people around me—our team, everybody. I'm super, super thankful and happy."

Sexton's crown means a great deal to everyone at Team Honda HRC and American Honda—even more than such an accomplishment normally would; although Honda has the most AMA Supercross race wins of any manufacturer (228, or 44 more than second place), the premier-class AMA Supercross title has eluded them since Ricky Carmichael earned it 20 years ago. That said, this is the 16th time that Honda has won the title (a record), with past Honda champions including such legends as Donnie Hansen, David Bailey, Johnny O'Mara, Rick Johnson, Jeff Stanton, Jean-Michel Bayle, Jeremy McGrath and Carmichael.

This marks only the third time that a manufacturer has won all three AMA Supercross Championships in the same season, with one of the other two also having been accomplished by Honda; in 1991, Team Honda's Bayle topped the premier class, with Peak/Pro Circuit Honda's McGrath and Brian Swink taking the West and East crowns, respectively. This latest title sweep marks the first time that it has been accomplished by one team, and Honda also collected the 2023 AMA Supercross Manufacturers Championship for the third consecutive time. In addition, Team Honda HRC rider Colt Nichols took the 2023 AMA 450SX Rookie of the Year Award. This all comes during a season in which Honda marks the 50th anniversary of its first production motocross bike, the CR250M Elsinore, which Gary Jones rode to Honda's first AMA Motocross Championship in 1973. 🔋

Recon?

TOM SEVERIN
4x4
Coach

Time for a little short-but-sweet tough love.

Four-wheeling involves near constant decision making. Numerous challenges face you along the trail. Whether you successfully navigate around or through those obstacles falls entirely on your shoulders.

Sorry, my friend, but you can't blame anyone else. Not your spotter. Not your mechanic. Not the fellow camper who messed up breakfast that morning.

Some 99% of all mistakes are caused by the driver. (The remaining 1% can be blamed on testosterone poisoning. But I'll leave that for another article.)

It all boils down to:

• Your assessment: How well you evaluated the obstacle.

• Your decision (go or no go): Most obstacles can be overcome. But sometimes you need to back away.

• Your execution: How well you implement the driving techniques required to successfully negotiate around or through that obstacle.

Follow the fundamentals of four-wheeling

Four-wheeling offers unique circumstances every moment. Sure, city driving has its hazards: screaming police vehicles, major road construction, zombie cab drivers, an occasional pile up. But you get used to those. Off road, it's a different story. You have to learn to expect the unexpected. And act accordingly.

Because every situation is unique, there are no cookbooks to guide you. Adhering to sound principles and executing properly will ensure a successful 4WD adventure.

All driving involves getting from Point A to Point B. Four-wheeling sets itself apart by constantly challenging drivers. For simplicity, I use the word

A flop

obstacles to refer to all challenges. Understand that doesn't mean just a large boulder. It could be a blind curve on a hillside. Or a narrow passageway through a brush-shrouded canyon.

You first must recognize the obstacle. That involves doing the recon. Four-wheeler's don't reconnoiter enough. My mantra is, recon, recon, recon.

Often that involves getting out of the vehicle and checking out the scene. Sometimes you can't see well enough through the windshield. Get out and walk up to the top of the hill or down to the bottom of slope. Whatever the situation calls for.

Next, decide on your path. That is, pick the line. Every obstacle off road has to be analyzed. Determine the best route to take; there could be more than one. You're looking for the one best suited to your vehicle.

How to pick the best line

As you analyze the situation, consider these four factors.

1. All four wheels must remain on the ground. If on a slope or mountainside, the vehicle could pitch slightly. Minimize the pitching or sideways sliding so all four wheels are available to you.

2. Verify clearance on all sides. Any rock outcroppings, branches, brush, or ruts that could hang up or damage your vehicle? Don't look in just one direction. Consider all angles: overhead, underneath and from either side.

3. Maintain traction. If driving on soft surfaces, adjust accordingly. You may have to air down, for example. Like point #1 above, you want to keep all four wheels working for you.

4. Use appropriate throttle. Don't go too fast or too slow. A good rule of thumb is: Go as slow as possible but as fast as necessary. Maintain that momentum.

Four-wheeling involves diligence on the driver's part. From assessing the situation to making the decision to executing. It's all about using the fundamentals properly. You as the driver are responsible for the successful execution of the trip. Keep driving, and over time you will develop the necessary skills.

As those skills develop, you will routinely make sound assessments and prudent decisions, and successfully execute those decisions.

P.S. While we're on the subject of decision making: Never try to help retrieve stuck vehicles by hanging or climbing on them. It is very hazardous to your health. We have safer ways to free them.

Tom Severin, 4x4 Coach, teaches 4WD owners how to confidently and safely use their vechicles to the fullest extent in difficult terrain and adverse driving conditions. Contact him at tom@4x4training.com or visit www.4x4training.com to develop or improve your driving skill. Copyright 2023, Badlands Off-Road Adventures, Inc

Beautiful sunset on the clouds 🌵

COMING EVENTS

CLEANUPS

CLEAN DEZERT
www.clean-dezert.org

KEEP OUR DESERT CLEAN
www.keepourdesertclean.com
Arizona Clean-ups
Jun 24, 2023 - Northern AZ or
Lake Cleanup
Sept 9, 2023 - West Valley
Cleanup
Nov 12, 2023 - Annual Volunteer
Appreciation Cleanup

LAND/UDG 760-791-1856

SAN DIEGO OFF ROAD COALITION
www.sdorc.org - info@sdorc.org

DESERT RACING

AMA DISTRICT 37
www.district37ama.org
Motorcycles & Quads
Jun 24, 2023 - Desert MC Night
Team Race, Red Mountain
Jul 15, 2023 - Lost Angels/4Aces
Night Team Race, Red Mountain
Sept 9, 2023 - Prairie Dogs MC
Night Team Race, Glen Helen
Sept 16, 2023 - Lost Coyotes
Desert Srambles, Red Mountain
Oct 21-22, 2023 - 100's MC Hare
& Hound, Johnson Valley
Nov 5, 2023 - Cactus Cats MC
Desert Scramble, Johnson Valley
Nov 18-19, 2023 - Hilltoppers MC
TT, 29 Palms

AMA DISTRICT 38
www.amad38.com
Races held near El Centro CA
Motorcycles & Quads
Sept 3, 2023 - D38 Grand Prix,
Glen Helen, San Bernardino CA
Sept 30, 2023 - Roadrunner
Rattlesnake Chase, Superstition
OHV Area
Oct 28, 2023 - I8 Monster Mash,
Superstition OHV Area
Nov 18, 2023 - Full Throttle
Veterans Day Dash, Lakebed
Dec 9, 2023 - Roadrunner
Christmas Classic, Plaster City
East

UTVs
Oct 8, 2023 - I8 Monster Mash,
Superstition
Nov 18, 2023 - Full Throttle
Veterans Day Dash, Lakebed
Dec 9, 2023 - Roadrunner
Christmas Classic, Plaster City East

AMA NATIONAL HARE & HOUND
www.NationalHareandHound.com
Motorcycles & Quads
Sept 9, 2023 - Round 5,
Panaca NV

Oct 21-22, 2023 - Round 6,
Lucerne Valley CA

AMA WEST HARE SCRAMBLES
www.westharescramble.com
Motorcycles & Quad
2023 Tentative Schedule
Jun 3-4, 2023 - Round 4,
Heppner OR
Jun 17-18, 2023 - Round 5,
Bellingham WA
TBA - Round 6
Oct 7-8, 2023 - Round 7,
Washougal WA
Nov 18-19, 2023 - Round 8,
Wilseyville CA

AMRA ARIZONA MOTORCYCLE RIDERS ASSOCIATION
www.amraracing.com
Motorcycle Racing
Sept 30 - Round 7, Hare
Scramble, Zeniff AZ
Oct 1, 2023 - Ropund 8, Hare
Scramble, Zeniff AZ

ARIZONA OFF ROAD PROMOTIONS
www.azopracing.com
Jul 22-23, 2023 - Cinder Mountain
Offroad Challenge, Flagstaff AZ
Oct 21, 2023 - Halloween Howler
Team Race, Cottonwood AZ

BEST IN THE DESERT
www.bitd.com
Aug 16-20, 2023 - Vegas to Reno
MC, Quad, UTV, Truck, Car
Oct 12-15, 2023 - Laughlin Desert
Challenge, 4WheelParts Youth
Series Event *MC, Quad, UTV,
Truck, Car*
Nov 9-12, 2023 - UTV Legends
Championship, 4WheelParts
Youth Series Event *MC, Quad,
UTV*

CODE OFF ROAD
www.codeoffroad.com.mx
Aug 4-6, 2023 - Tersa Grand Prix,
Tecate B.C.
Oct 13-15, 2023 - Mexlog 300,
Mexicali B.C.
Dec 15-17, 2023 - Polaris Baja
275, Mexicali - San Felipe B.C.

LEGACY RACING
www.legacyracing.net
June 23-25, 2023 - UTV Freedom
Ride
Sept 22-24, 2023 - Dirt
Rebelution, Cedar City UT *MC/
Quad/UTV*
Oct 19-22, 2023 - Gold Rush,
Virginia City to Tonopah NV *Cars/
Trucks/MC/Quad/UTV*

Nov 30-Dec 3, 2023 - Stateline
Shootout, Primm NV *Cars/
Trucks/UTV*

M.O.R.E. www.moreracing.net
Cars, Trucks and UTVs
Jul 8, 2023 - GG Lighting
Freedom Cup, Glen Helen, San
Bernardino CA
Sept 23, 2023 - PCI Race Radios
300, Johnson Valley CA
Dec 2, 2023 - Transaxle
Engineering Challenge,
Barstow CA

NORRA www.norra.com

RECORD OFF ROAD
www.recordoffroad.com
Jun 23-25, 2023 - Ens-San Felipe
250
Oct 6-8, 2023 - Ens - Ens 350
Dec 8-10, 2023 - Race Ready
250

SCORE
www.score-international.com
Sept 12-17, 2023 - 4th SCORE
Baja 400, Ensenada
Nov 13-18, 2023 - 56th SCORE
Baja 1000, La Paz

SNORE www.snoreracing.net
Jun 9-10, 2023 - Barstow 2
Vegas, Barstow/Jean
Oct 20-21, 2023 - Ridgecrest,
Ridgecrest CA
Dec 8-10, 2023 - Rage at the
River, Laughlin NV

SADR - Southern Arizona Desert Racing
www.racesadr.com
Sept 22-23, 2023 - Point to Point
Dec 1-2, 2023 - Cholla 250

VORRA www.vorraracing.com
Jul 14-16, 2023 - The Dog Fight
250, Fallon NV
Sept 3-4, 2023 - The Stomping
Grounds 300, Yerington NV
Oct 19-23, 2023 - Gold Rush,
Virginia City - Tonopah NV

ZR PROMOTIONS
(686) 564-6653
www.zrpromo.com
Motorcycles, Quads and UTVs
Jul 1, 2023 - Desafio Premiers
Nite Race, Mexicali B.C.

DUAL SPORT

BIG BEAR TRAIL RIDERS MC
www.bigbeartrailriders.com
Jun 24-25, 2023 - Big Bear
Run, Big Bear Mountain Ski
Resort

CRAWDAD OFF ROAD EVENTS
www.crawdadoffroadevents.com
Sept 22-25, 2023 - Bar 10 Ranch,
Mesquite NV

D-37 DUAL SPORT
www.district37ama.org/dualsport/
Jun 5, 2023 - 3rd Annual Gold
Rush 150, Lebec CA

DUAL SPORT WEST
www.dualsportwest.com
Jun 11-15, 2023 - New GWT
Second Section, Williams AZ
Aug 19-26, 2023 - Mex2Can
Second Half, Fallon NV
Aug 22-28, 2023 - New GWT Third
Section, Park City UT
Sept 23-24, 2023 - Mammoth 300,
Mammoth Lakes CA
Sept 23-24, 2023 - Topaz 400,
Topaz NV
Oct 14-15, 2023 - Prescott 300,
Prescott AZ
Oct 27-29, 2023 - China Lake 300,
Ridgecrest CA
Oct 28-29, 2023 - Lone Pine 300,
Lone Pine CA

DUST DEVILS MC
www.dustdevilsmc.com

FAMILY OFF ROAD ADVENTURES
www.familyoffroadadventures.com
209-649-3633
Jul 20-24, 2023 - Coast to Crater
Adventure, Fort Bragg CA

ORANGE COUNTY DUALIES
www.dualies.com
Jul 29-30, 2023 - Kennedy
Meadows Dual Sport Ride
(current club members only)
Sept 29, 2023 - Santiago Peak
Club ride (current club members
only)

SAN DIEGO ADVENTURE RIDERS
www.dualsport-sd.com

VENTURA COUNTY M/C CLUB
www.venturacountymc.com

ENDURANCE

GLEN HELEN
www.glenhelen.com
Jun 10, 2023 - 3 Bros 10 Hour
Endurance Race
Oct 7-8, 2023 - 3 Bros 24 Hour
Endurance Race

ENDUROCROSS

GEICO AMA ENDUROCROSS
www.endurocross.com

ENDUROS

AMRA
www.amraracing.com
Jun 4, 2023 - Round 6, Enduro,
Flagstaff AZ

DISTRICT 37
www.district37ama.org
Sept 23, 2023 - D37 Co Op Sprint
Enduro, Red Mountain

LOS ANCIANOS MC CLUB
www.losancianos.com

REDDING DIRT RIDERS
www.reddingdirtriders.com

FLAT TRACK

AMERICAN FLAT TRACK
www.americanflattrack.com
Jun 17, 2023 - Du Quoin Mile,
Du Quoin IL
Jun 24, 2023 - Bridgeport Half-
Mile, Middletown NJ
Jul 1, 2023 - West Virginia Half-
Mile, Mineral Wells WV
Jul 8, 2023 - Orange County Half-
Mile, Middletown NY
Jul 22, 2023 - Bridgeport Half-
Mile, Bridgeport NJ
Jul 30, 2023 - SC2 Peoria TT,
Peoria IL
Aug 6, 2023 - Buffalo Chip TT,
Sturgis SD
Aug 12, 2023 - Castle Rock TT,
Castle Rock WA
Sept 2-3, 2023 - Springfield Mile
I&II, Springfield IL

AZ FLAT TRACK RACING
www.azflattrackracing.com
Sept 9, 2023 - Adobe Mountain
Speedway
Sept 23, 2023 - Adobe Mountain
Speedway
Oct 7, 2023 - Adobe Mountain
Speedway
Oct 21, 2023 - Adobe Mountain
Speedway
Nov 4, 2023 - Adobe Mountain
Speedway
Nov 18, 2023 - Adobe Mountain
Speedway

AZ SOUTHLAND FLAT TRACK
@Azsouthland_flattrack
480-688-5278
All races held at South Buckeye
Equestrian & Event Center,
Buckeye AZ
June 10, 2023 - Round 6

CALVMX FLAT TRACK
www.calvmx.net
Camp Lockett, Campo CA
Jun 24-25, 2023 - Round 2
Jul 22-23, 2023 - Round 3
Aug 26-27, 2023 - Round 4

SAN DIEGO OFF ROAD COALITION

DIRT TALK RADIO

WWW.SDORC.ORG

With Ed Stovin, Audrey Mason
& Dave Stall

THE ANSWER
FM 96.1 | AM 1170
NORTH COUNTY | SAN DIEGO

EVERY SUNDAY 12-1 P.M. PST

Sept 23-24, 2023 - Round 5
Oct 28-29, 2023 - Round 6
Nov 18-19, 2023 - Round 7

KERN RACEWAY
www.kernraceway.com
Sept 16, 2023 - Professional
Speedway and Flat Track
Oct 14, 2023 - AMA U21 National
Speedway Championships and
Flat Track
Nov 4, 2023 - AMA Professional
Speedway Pairs Championship
and Flat Track
Dec 2, 2023 - FIM North
American Speedway Final and
Flat track

**EVENTS SUBJECT TO
CANCELLATION OR ERROR**

LAKE ELSINORE MX PARK
www.facebook.com/
Lake-Elsinore-Motorsports-
Park-104247691683693/
Flat track open for practice on
weekends. No knobbies.

**SOUTHERN CALIFORNIA FLAT
TRACK ASSOCIATION**
www.southerncalifornia
flattrack.com
All races held at Perris Raceway,
Perris CA
Jun 3-4, 2023 - Rounds 6&7
Sept 16, 2023 - Round 8
Oct 7, 2023- Round 9
Nov 11-12, 2023 - Rounds 10&11
Dec 9, 2023 - Round 12

WESTERN FLAT TRACK
www.westernflattrack.com

4WD CLUBS/EVENTS
**BADLANDS OFF ROAD
ADVENTURES**
www.4x4training.com

**CALIFORNIA 4WD
ASSOCIATION INC.**
www.cal4wheel.com
Aug 10-13, 2023 - Sierra Trek,
near Truckee CA
Sept 1-4, 2023 - High Sierra
Poker Run, near Shaver Lake CA
Oct 13-14, 2023 - Operation
Desert Fun, Ocotillo Wells CA
Nov 10-12, 2023 - Panamint
Valley Days, near Trona CA

CAPO VALLEY 4 WHEELERS
www.cv4w.org

DESERT SIDE TRACS
www.dst4x4club.org

DIABLO 4-WHEELERS
www.diablo4wheelers.com
Jun 3-4, 2023 - The Gargoyles,
Stanislaus NF
Jun 8-11, 2023 - Rubicon Run
Jun 30-Jul 5, 2023 - Bear Valley
Loop Trail Opening and July 4th
Jul 8-16, 2023 - SlickRock Week
Aug 10-13, 2023 - Sierra Trek
Aug 15-20, 2023 - Fordyce/
Meadow Lake

EARLY BRONCOS LTD
www.earlybronco.com

GEARED FOUR FUN 4WD CLUB
www.geared4fun.com

HEMET JEEP CLUB
www.hemetjeepclub.com

**INLAND EMPIRE FOUR
WHEELRS**
www.ie4w.com

JUSTRUNS www.justruns.com

PARKER 4 WHEELERS
www.parker4wheelers.net

**POINT MUGU 4WD
CLUB, INC.**
www.pointmugu4wd.org

COMING EVENTS

RED ROCK 4-WHEELERS
www.rr4w.com
Mar 23-31, 2024 - Easter Jeep
Safari 2024, Moab UT

SAN DIEGO 4 WHEELERS
www.sd4wheel.com
Jul 10-16, 2023 - Out of State
Run to San Juan Mountains CO

**SAN DIEGO OUTBACKS
4X4 CLUB**
(760) 789-8294

SCOUTS WEST 4WDC
www.scoutswest.com
Apr 2024 - IH Western Regionals,
Calico CA

**SONS OF THUNDER
4-WHEELERS**
www.sonsofthunder4x4.com
Jun 24, 2023 - Cleghorn
Jul 22, 2023 - Pilot Rock
Aug 18-2023 - Big Bear

TIERRA DEL SOL
www.tds4x4.com

VEGAS VALLEY 4 WHEELERS
www.vv4w.org

VICTOR VALLEY 4 WHEELERS
www.victorvalley4wheelers.com

**WILLYS OVERLAND
MOAB RALLY**
www.willysrally.com

EVENTS SUBJECT TO CANCELLATION OR ERROR

4WD TRAINING
**BADLANDS OFF ROAD
ADVENTURES**
www.4x4training.com
June 3, 2023 - Tire Repair And
Hi-Lift Clinic
June 17, 2023 - Staring Rock
Crawling
June 23, 2023 - OAUSA Field
Day

FUN RUNS
CORVA www.corva.org

**MORONGO BASIN SEARCH &
RESCUE** - www.desertrun.org

REDDING DIRT RIDERS
www.reddingdirtriders.com

**SAN DIEGO OFF ROAD
COALITION**
www.sdorc.org

SOBOBA RIDES, San Jacinto CA
www.sobobarides.biz

UTV Off Road Adventures
www.utvoffroad
adventures.com

G.P.'S
AMA DISTRICT 37
www.district37ama.org
Sept 30-Oct 1, 2023 - Viewfinders
GP
Oct 13-15, 2023 - Vikings MC

AMA DISTRICT 38
www.amad38.com
Sept 3, 2023 - D38 Grand Prix,
Glen Helen Raceway, San
Bernardino CA

AMRA
www.amraracing.com
Nov 4, 2023 - Round 9, Vicksburg
AZ

**ARIZONA OFF ROAD
PROMOTIONS**
www.azopracing.com
Jul 8-9, 2023 - Mormon Lake
Grand Prix, Mormon Lake AZ
Oct 7-8, 2023 -

FIRE & POLICE MOTOCROSS
www.firepolicemx.com
Dec 5, 2023 - Christmas GP,
Lake Elsinore Motorsports Park,
Lake Elsinore CA

GLEN HELEN, Devore CA
www.glenhelen.com
Jun 25, 2023 - Round 6 SRA
Jul 23, 2023 - Round 7 SRA
Aug 27, 2023 - Round 8 SRA
Sept 24, 2023 - Round 9 SRA
Oct 22, 2023 - Round 10 SRA
Nov 19, 2023 - Round 11 SRA
Dec 10, 2023 - Round 12 SRA

LACR MX, Palmdale CA
www.lacr.mx

**NATIONAL GRAND PRIX
SERIES**
www.ngpcseries.com
Aug 18-20, 2023 - Round 8,
Preston ID

Sept 30-Oct 1, 2023 - Round 9,
Ridgecrest CA
Nov 10-12, 2023 - Lake Havasu
AZ

REDDING DIRT RIDERS
www.reddingdirtriders.com

SRA www.sragp.com
Motorcycles, Quads, UTVs
All events held at Glen Helen,
San Bernardino CA
Jun 25, 2023 - Round 6
Jul 23, 2023 - Round 7
Aug 27, 2023 - Round 8
Sept 24, 2023 - Round 9
Oct 22, 2023 - Round 10
Nov 19, 2023 - Round 11
Dec 10, 2023 - Round 12

**VIRGINIA CITY MOTORSPORTS
CLUB**
www.vcgp.com
Apr 27-28, 2024 - Virginia City
Grand Prix, Virginia City NV

ZR PROMOTIONS
www.zrpromo.com

MOTOCROSS
*Also see Vintage Motocross
Category*

2X PROMOTIONS
www.2xpromotions.com
Jun 2, 2023 - Loretta
Lynn's Southwest Regional
Championship, Pala CA
Jun 9, 2023 - Loretta Lynn's
Midwest Regional Championship,
Rancho Cordova CA

Jun 16, 2023 - Mammoth
Motocross 2023, Mammoth
Lakes CA

**AMA AMATEUR NATIONAL MX
REGIONAL**
www.mxsports.com
Southwest Area Qualifier
Jun 2-4, 2023 - Southwest
Regional, Fox Raceway, Pala
CA
Jul 31-Aug 5, 2023 - National
Championship, Hurricane
Mills TN

**AMA LUCAS OIL PRO MX
CHAMPIONSHIP**
www.mxnationals.com
Jun 3, 2023 - Prairie City SVRA,
Rancho Cordova CA
Jun 10, 2023 - Thunder Valley
MX Park, Lakewood CO
Jul 1, 2023 - RedBud MX,
Buchanan MI
Jul 8, 2023 - The Wick 338,
Southwick MA
Jul 15, 2023 - Spring Creek MX
Park, Millville MN
Aug 12, 2023 - Unadilla MX, New
Berlin NY
Aug 19, 2023 - Budds Creek MX
Park, Mechanicsville MD
Aug 26, 2023 - Ironman Raceway,
Crawfordsville IN

AME MINICROSS
www.ameminicross.com
All events held at Glen Helen
Raceway, San Bernardino CA

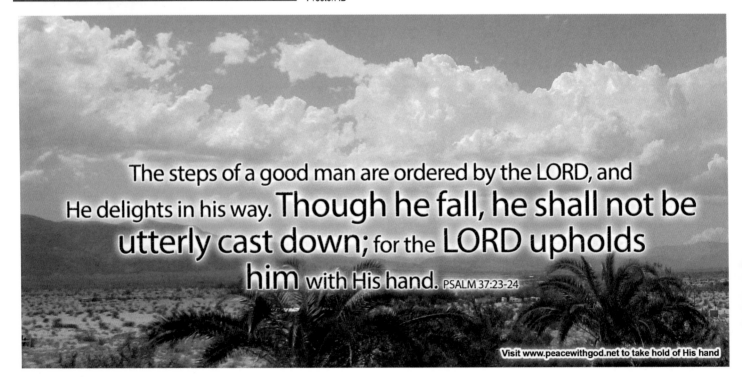

The steps of a good man are ordered by the LORD, and He delights in his way. Though he fall, he shall not be utterly cast down; for the LORD upholds him with His hand. PSALM 37:23-24

Visit www.peacewithgod.net to take hold of His hand

CAHUILLA CREEK MX
Anza CA
www.cahuillacreek
motocross.com

DT1 MX Park Tulare CA
www.dt1mxpark.com

FIRE & POLICE MOTOCROSS
www.firepolicemx.com
Jun 12, 2023 - Round 3, Glen
Helen, San Bernardino CA
Oct 9-10, 2023 - Rounds 4&5,
Lake Elsinore Motorsports Park

FOX RACEWAY Pala CA
raceway.palatribe.com

GLEN HELEN RACEWAY
Devore CA
www.glenhelen.com

LA PLAYA MOTOCROSS
Rosarito, Mexico
www.facebook.com/
laplayamotocross

LACR MX, Palmdale CA
www.lacr.mx

MOTO 4 KIDS
www.moto4kids.racing
Rad Riders Series
Jun 10, 2023 - Summer School
Series #1, Pala CA
Jul 8, 2023 - Summer School
Series #2, Pala CA
Aug 5, 2023 - Summer School
Series #3, Pala CA
Aug 27, 2023 - Rad Riders Series
#1, Pala CA
Sept 17,, 2023 - Rad Riders
Series #2, Tulare CA
Oct 8, 2023 - Rad Riders Series
#3, Pala CA
Nov 12, 2023 - Rad Riders Series
#4, Lakeside CA
Dec 10, 2023 - Rad Riders Series
#5, Pala CA

**OLD SCHOOL SCRAMBLES
RACING**
www.ossrg.org
All races held at Glen Helen
Raceway, San Bernardino CA
Jun 4, 2023 - TT Scrambles
Series Round 4
Jul 16, 2023 - TT Scrambles
Series Round 5

OVER THE HILL GANG
www.overthe hillgang.org
Jun 18, 2023 - OTHG Classic,
Glen Helen
Aug 6, 2023 - Hosted by OTMX,
LACR
Aug 13, 2023 - Triple Crown
Series Rd 1, Lake Elsinore
Sept 2-3, 2023 - Bay National,
Day 1&2, Argyll MX
Sept 17, 2023 - Triple Crown
Series Rd 2, Lake Elsinore
Oct 1, 2023 - OTHG CA
Championship, DT1 MX
Oct 15, 2023 - Triple Crown
Series Rd 3, Lake Elsinore

PERRIS RACEWAY
Perris CA
www.rideperris.com

SOCAL OLD TIMERS MX CLUB
www.socalotmx.org
Jun 4, 2023 - Glen Helen, San
Bernardino CA
Jun 11, 2023 - Cahuilla, Anza CA
Jun 25, 2023 - Elsinore, Lake
Elsinore CA

**SOCAL CHAMPIONSHIP
MOTOCROSS**
www.socalmxseries.com

WMN RACING
www.wmnracing.org

WORCS www.worcsracing.com
Bikes/Quads/SXS
Sept 15-17, 2023 - R7, Vernal UT
Oct 6-8, 2023 - R8, Mesquite NV
Oct 20-22, 2023 - R9, Primm NV

OFF ROAD RALLY
SONORA RALLY
www.sonorarally.com

OFF ROAD SHOWS
OFF ROAD EXPO
www.offroadexpo.com
Sept 30 - Oct 1, 2023 - Off Road
Expo, Pomona CA
Oct 14-15, 2023 - Off Road Expo,
Phoenix AZ

SAND SPORTS SUPER SHOW
www.sandsports supershow.com
Sept 15-17 2023 - eBay Motors
Sand Sports Super Show, Costa
Mesa CA

**SAN DIEGO OFF ROAD
COALITION**
www.sdorc.org
Jun 24, 2023 - Off Road
Jamboree, Lakeside CA

ROCK CRAWLING
**DIRT RIOT ENDURANCE
RACING**
www.werocklive.com
Western Series
Jun 24-25, 2023 - Round 3,
Vernal UT
Jul 29-30, 2023 - Round
4, Broken Boulder Farm,
Goldendale WA

NOR CAL ROCK RACING
www.norcalrockracing.com
Jun 23, 2023 - King Shocks
NorCal Finals, Prairie City SVRA

ULTRA 4 RACING
www.ultra4racing.com

SAND DRAGS
SOCAL SAND DRAGS
www.socalsanddrags.com
Jun 9-11, 2023 - SCSDA Summer
Showdown, Lake Elsinore
Motorsports, Lake Elsinore CA

SHORT COURSE
**GREAT AMERICAN
SHORTCOURSE**
www.greatamericanshort
course.com
Jun 10-11, 2023 - Rounds 4&5,
SBC Fairgrounds, Victorville CA
Oct 6-8, 2023 - Rounds 6&7,
Primm Raceway, Primm NV
Nov 4-5, 2023 - Rounds 8&9,
SBC Fairgrounds, Victorville CA

**SPEED ENERGY FORMULA
OFF ROAD**
www.stadium supertrucks.com
Aug 4-6, 2023 - Nashville TN

SPEEDWAY
COSTA MESA SPEEDWAY
www.costamesaspeedway.net
Jun 17, 2023 - Harley Night #2,
Speedway, Sidecars
Sept 9, 2023 - Harley Night
Finals, Speedway, Sidecars
Sept 23, 2023 - 53rd United
States National Speedway
Championship
Sept 30, 2023 - Fall Classic,
Speedway, Sidecars, Juniors

KERN RACEWAY
www.kernraceway.com
Jun 24, 2023 - AMA Professional
Speedway Championship
Sept 16, 2023 - Professional
Speedway and Flat Track
Oct 14, 2023 - AMA U21 National
Speedway Championships and
Flat Track
Nov 4, 2023 - AMA Professional
Speedway Pairs Championship
and Flat Track
Dec 2, 2023 - FIM North
American Speedway Final and
Flat Track

SUPERCROSS
**MONSTER ENERGY
SUPERCROSS**
www.supercrosslive.com

TRIALS
AHRMA www.ahrma.org

**SOUTHERN CALIFORNIA
TRIALS ASSOCIATION**
www.socaltrials.com

VINTAGE MX
AHRMA www.ahrma.org
National Vintage MX Series
Jun 10, 2023 - Grand Cane LA
Jun 17, 2023 - Moberly MO

AMERICAN RETROCROSS
www.americanretrocross.org
Jun 18, 2023 - Glen Helen
Raceway, San Bernardino CA
Jul 30, 2023 - Glen Helen
Raceway, San Bernardino CA
Sept 17, 2023 - Glen Helen
Raceway, San Bernardino CA
Oct 15, 2023 - Glen Helen
Raceway, San Berrnardino CA
Dec 3, 2023 - Glen Helen
Raceway, San Bernardino CA

**AMERICAN VINTAGE DIRT
RACERS ASSOCIATION**
www.avdra.com
Jun 25, 2023 - Race 6, Bull
Hollow Raceeway, Monticello UT
Oct 15, 2023 - Race 7, Motoland,
Casa Grande AZ
Nov 12, 2023 - Race 8, Motoland,
Casa Grande AZ
Dec 10, 2023 - Race 9, Shorty's
Sports Park, Blythe CA

CALVMX www.calvmx.net
Jun 11, 2023 - Round 2, Perris CA
Jul 9, 2023 - Round 3, Perris CA
Sept 10, 2023 - Round 4, Perris
CA
Oct 21, 2023 - Scott Burnworth's
SoCal MX Classic Event, Glen
Helen Raceway

ADVERTISER

Please make these companies your first choice for off road purchases.
They're the ones who bring you this magazine!

INDEX

PHOTO Scenery captured at the AMA District 38 Easter Scrambles race in 2016. Photo by Judd Neves Nothing But Dirt Racing Photography

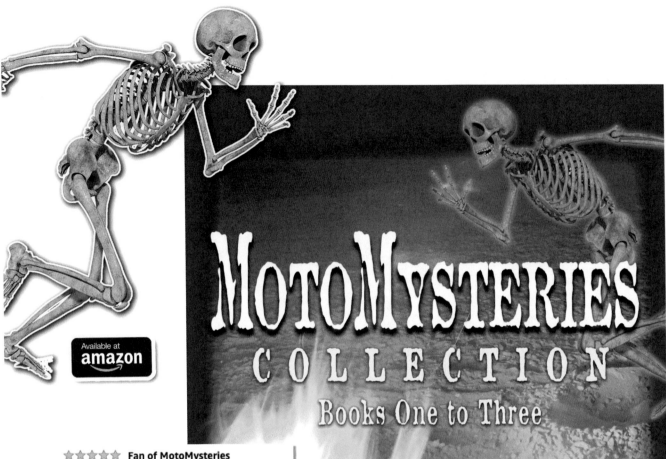

MotoMysteries
COLLECTION
Books One to Three

★★★★★ **Fan of MotoMysteries**
Reviewed in the United States on May 11, 2021

Great gift, or just for getting your kids to read. Kids love to read books that grab their attention and get their imaginations growing. These books do both , and adults like them too. Love the 3 in 1 set! Not just for off road families, but opens awareness of desert living and the love of foster families! Win Win!
- Lisa Kincaid
Amazon Reviewer

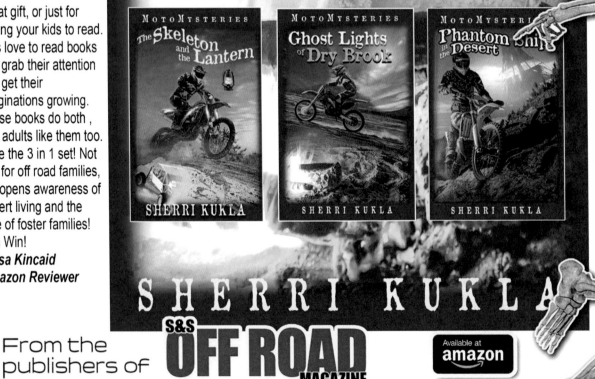

SHERRI KUKLA

From the publishers of **S&S OFF ROAD MAGAZINE**

Made in the USA
Las Vegas, NV
07 June 2023

73076463R00062